The Challenge of Nuclear Terror

The Challenge of Nuclear Terror

Sitakanta Mishra

KNOWLEDGE WORLD

KW Publishers Pvt Ltd

in association with

Centre for Air Power Studies

The **Centre for Air Power Studies** is an independent, non-profit, academic research institution established in 2002 under a registered Trust to undertake and promote policy-related research, study and discussion on the trends and developments in defence and military issues, especially air power and the aerospace arena, for civil and military purposes. Its publications seek to expand and deepen the understanding of defence, military power, air power and aerospace issues without necessarily reflecting the views of any institution or individuals except those of the authors.

Jasjit Singh
Director
Centre for Air Power Studies
P-284, Arjan Path
Subroto Park
New Delhi 110010

Tele: (91-11) 25699131
E-mail: office@aerospaceindia.org

KNOWLEDGE WORLD

KW Publishers Pvt Ltd
5A/4A Ansari Road, Daryaganj, New Delhi 110002

Published in India by Kalpana Sukhla, KW Publishers Pvt Ltd

ISBN 10: 81-87966-90-4
ISBN 13: 978-81-87966-90-6

Typeset by Black Innovation, New Delhi and printed at Raj Kamal Electric Press

Contents

Foreword

The gravest danger to the present world lies in radicalism and misuse of technology. While extremist groups have been splintered all over, technology has been diffused to every nook and corner. To the new world that now we have entered, our previous understanding about defence and deterrence no longer fully applies and this is more so post-9/11. The phenomenon of nuclear terrorism needs to be looked at from this perspective. It is evident that terrorists have shown interest in nuclear technology but have not yet achieved any major breakthrough. But any complacency, owing to the unavailability of a nuclear terror precedent, and the prevailing gap between terrorist aspirations and capabilities, is fallacious.

By now, the threat of a global nuclear war is near zero. The danger that we face today is not regarding the fate of the earth but the fate of our cities. There exists widespread apprehension these days on the probable slippage of radiological materials into the hands of the rogue non-state actors. This apprehension, in a way, is obvious; the fact is, the perceived benefits that motivate states to acquire these arsenals are equally lucrative for the non-state actors. As radiological materials are used in numerous sectors, the fear arises that terrorists may get hold of these materials to fabricate a radiological dispersal device (RDD) or "dirty bomb" which can be carried in a suitcase and exploded in a crowded city. Though fabrication of a full-fledged nuclear arsenal is extremely difficult as it requires state-level resources which terrorists may not be able to mobilise, they can effectively exploit the negative public perception on anything nuclear. Therefore, the danger of nuclear terror, explicitly or implicitly, is existent, even if the probability of its occurrence is remote.

The global nuclear discourse is now at a turning point where two explicit trends are axiomatic. While, on the one hand, it has been established that nuclear weapons cannot be used as an instrument of war, on the other, a consensus for global nuclear disarmament is gradually being reached. Therefore, "a renewed nuclear debate", as Sitakanta argues for in the first chapter, is certainly "overdue". The emergence of non-state actors as a stable entity of international discourse, and their capabilities, strategy and expanse necessitate an urgent review of the security providing role of nuclear weapons. Also, the concept of deterrence requires a revisit, to which Sitakanta's "neo-deterrence" proposition fits in.

Nuclear terrorism seems to be an immediate challenge for the whole world and more so for India which harbours a sizeable nuclear infrastructure dispersed across its territory. The country has also been a victim of terrorism for many decades. A public discussion on the possibility of a nuclear terror incident might generate panic. However, the phenomenon is an uncertain reality; experts need to study it, policy-makers need to respond to it, and the public also urgently needs to be educated to deal with such an emergency, if ever it takes place. In this perspective, the second chapter of the study rightly highlights the vulnerability of the Indian nuclear infrastructure, the probability of a terror incident, and the preparedness of India to deal with such a situation.

India has an impeccable record of safeguarding its radioactive materials and infrastructure. Since it is planning to expand its nuclear infrastructure to meet its energy requirements, its safety and security must be the top priority. Any complacency thereof is unwarranted. The present global concern about the safety of nuclear facilities, especially post-9/11, has effectively been reflected upon India. The scientific community, in the aftermath of 9/11, has been known to have undertaken an extensive review of the safety structure and preparedness of the mechanisms in place. Considering the gravity of the terrorists' spread, their capability and motives, a nuclear terror incident can be conceivable as a worst case scenario.

FOREWORD

A nuclear terror incident should not, and may not, take place, but a final word on terrorism is impossible. As eternal vigilance is vital for security, not only a heightened safety approach but a concerted effort, involving civilians, defence, the scientific community and government authority, as Sitakanta is proposing, is the need of the hour. India has advanced a lot in this direction, but much more needs to be done. His proposals for an effective Nuclear Information Management (NIM) system and strengthening of the medical infrastructure are worthy of serious consideration.

I take immense pleasure in penning these few lines and wish him all success. His thoughts are very relevant, and I hope this book will trigger a fission of such thoughts in terms of debates, writings and seminal studies.

Air Cmdr. Jasjit Singh (Retd.)

Acknowledgements

In the process of writing this paper I have accumulated a series of intellectual debts. First of all, Dr. Manpreet Sethi has been an invaluable source of inspiration and support. She has extended unstinting guidance all along. I am immensely grateful to Air Commodore Jasjit Singh, AVM Kapil Kak and Brigadier Gurmeet Kanwal for giving valuable insights during my interaction with them. They have provided uninterrupted support and guidance in spite of their busy schedules. Also, my interaction with many distinguished air force officers at the Centre for Air Power Studies (CAPS) was extremely helpful in building up the study.

I have benefited immensely from the discussions with my friends Vinod Stuti, Ajaya, Shelly, Garima, Rajasimman, Monika and Ginny. They have been my constant source of inspiration; in many ways, they were in fact the motivating forces to complete the work. I am thankful to the CAPS library, especially librarian Shweta Dhingra who has extended generous, unhesitant support in locating the study materials.

I must acknowledge the invisible hands of many writers on the subject in helping me to conceptualise and speculate on the subject, Charles D. Ferguson, Rajesh M. Basrur, P.R. Chari, Seema Gehlaut, Manpreet Sethi, etc. to name a few. I have borrowed heavily ideas from their writings. I am extremely thankful to Dr. Savita Pande for her valuable inputs and encouragement to finish the study.

In my understanding, speculation is an integral part of security analyses.

Beside other things, the specificity of a strategic thinker lies in extracting the facts and thinking the unthinkable. Here an attempt is made to dig out the nuances of nuclear politics and defy the conventional wisdom. However, the endeavour was not easy owing to the fact that accessing authentic information on the security structure of Indian nuclear facilities is extremely difficult; therefore, the study is mainly based on open source information and personal interaction with eminent Indian nuclear scientists. Also, the intention here is not to generate havoc. The Indian nuclear infrastructure is relatively safe and the security system in and around the facilities is comparatively good. It is only attempted here to bring into notice the existing loopholes and probable threats to strengthen their safety further.

Sitakanta Mishra

1

From Security by Nuclear Weapons to Security of Nuclear Weapons

A Renewed Nuclear Debate is Long Overdue

Acquiring weapons and materials is the hardest step for the terrorists to take, and the easiest step for us to stop. By contrast, every subsequent step in the process – building the bomb, transporting it, and detonating it – is easier for the terrorists to take, and harder for us to stop.... No nuclear material, no nuclear weapon. No nuclear weapon, no nuclear terrorism.

– ***Charles B. Curtis***

Shut your eyes ...

...and imagine...... Al Qaeda manages to acquire a nuclear bomb ... it captures a part of the territory of, say, Pakistan's Balochistan, with the help of tribal insurgents and declares it a sovereign country. It also announces an election and threatens to use nuclear weapons if anybody (Pakistan, India, China or the US) intervenes in the process. The UN calls for an emergency Security Council meeting to which Pakistan is a special invitee. At the same time, India, Pakistan, Afghanistan and China suggest that the United States desist from any extreme action that could result in nuclear retaliation by Al Qaeda on the respective countries. The presidents of the US and Russia consult the Cold War dictionary to see if there is any reference to such a situation. No solution is found. The UN secretary general appeals to Al Qaeda to be rational. Osama bin Laden comes out with a bargain to the world to reverse all the nuclear doctrines and strategies. The entire world nuclear discourse is now in question. Strategic thinkers across the globe start investigating why their work could not come to the rescue in such a situation. Should they now consider revising deterrence theory, assign a new role to nuclear weapons, or adapt them to the changed global situation?

The above hypothetical narration vindicates how "the changed political conditions ... have converted nuclear weapons from queens on the chessboard of international politics into military and political hostages."[1] World nuclear discourse that revolves round state behaviour, needs fundamental rethinking now when non-state actors have emerged as rivals to the state domain. Nuclear weapons, doctrines and strategies require to be adapted to the new world order wherein non-state entities are a reality. One simple reason is that the "nuclear weapon has made the defender's job easy and the attacker's difficult." Though nuclear strategic doctrines and concepts developed in the Cold War years are not entirely irrelevant to the new geo-political global situation, these concepts require careful amendment and, in some cases, complete rethinking.

This paper is an attempt to underline the existing nuances in the present nuclear order. The arguments are based on the assumption that nuclear weapons are here to stay but their role as a security providers has been severely challenged owing to many peculiar global developments; if not timely reoriented, nuclear weapons would prove to be a burden on human civilisation. The major challenge to the nuclear discourse today is terrorism which might exploit the terror potential of nuclear weapons. The central thesis here is that the nuclear discourse seems to be moving from the era of *security by nuclear weapons to security of nuclear weapons,* and a new nuclear debate is imminent. This paper examines the probability of nuclear terrorism by analysing different options available for the terrorists to exploit the existing loopholes in the nuclear discourse and the security structure. It goes into the details of the changing global strategic situation, examines the various types and ways of nuclear terror, finally reaching the conclusion that a neo-deterrence framework (a new nuclear debate) is urgently needed to curb the chances of nuclear weapons, materials, knowhow, etc. falling into the hands of the terrorists.

I

Security by Nuclear Weapons

Quantification of security provided by nuclear weapons is difficult and has always been contentious. Even understanding why states go nuclear is a complex and critical excercise. Literature on the nuclear arming choice of states agrees on some overlapping factors that seem to propel a state to take the nuclear road. According to Scott D. Sagan, the first is the "security and fear model," the second is the "norms model," and the last is the "domestic politics model."[2] According to the security and fear model, states build nuclear weapons to enhance their security against external threats by enhancing their own bullying potential or for countering another country's bullying potential. The neo-realist argument supports the security model by asserting that states operate in an anarchical international system and, therefore, must rely on 'self-help' to protect their national sovereignty and security. Owing to their enormous destructive power, nuclear weapons have proved to be the ultimate source of security. However, the security model is not adequate to understand the nuclear arming behaviour of states. Domestic constituencies like the scientific-bureaucratic community, political parties, national leaders, and domestic public opinion play equally important roles in nuclear decision-making. The last is the norms model where Sagan argues that states sometimes pursue nuclear programmes primarily for their prestige value or grandeur.

Owing to this and many other reasons, states have piled up their nuclear arsenals without answering the question: "How much is enough?" Former US President Dwight Eisenhower was among the few to diagnose the ailment when he told his advisers, "We are piling up these armaments because we do not know what else to do to provide for our security."[3] Another contentious question of this debate is: does the expansion of the nuclear arsenal by a state really translate into additional security? The explanation is dyadic. While one group of strategists argues that in the shadow of the atomic bomb, the future of the world is "uncertain, fearful and dangerous," the other group is of the view that more nuclear weapons would ensure stability and security owing to the deterrent effects that lie in the eyes of the beholder.[4] There also exists a dichotomy between war prevention efforts and nuclear disarmament: nuclear weapons cannot be abolished until war is first done away with; the other way round, war will never be abolished as long as there are nuclear weapons. However, the nuclear weapons came into existence not in a vacuum. It was a so-called historical and circumstantial necessity. Even today, one and half a decades after the end of the Cold War, there are many justifications for the role of nuclear arsenals in the national security strategies.

There have been numerous instances in the past when nuclear weapons are claimed to have played a security-enhancing role. The United States, the first country to produce a nuclear bomb, was motivated by the fear that Germany would succeed in its quest for nuclear weapons, and that its own nuclear weapons were imperative to assure its own security and that of the Allied powers, by deterring the Germans from using theirs. The same country used nuclear bombs on Japan with the justification that it would "ensure speedy conclusion" of the war and "save thousands of American lives."[5] The next state to acquire the weapons was the Soviet Union under the pretext that the US would use its nuclear weapons to dominate it. Driven by the fear of US domination, Soviet leaders sought security in the deterrence potential of the weapons, while at the same time, adding to their prestige and bestowing upon themselves the bullying potential. Subsequently, Britain and France, both of which could have opted to remain under the US nuclear umbrella, chose instead to develop their own arsenals. This reasoning was said to be based on the fear that the US would not go to the extent of sacrificing New York in order to retaliate against a Soviet attack on London or Paris. Thus, both countries decided to develop their own nuclear weapons out of fear and lack of trust in the US nuclear umbrella. At the same time, by becoming nuclear weapon states, they could bolster their waning prestige in the world. China followed suit, fearing that without nuclear weapons, its security would be threatened by both the US and Soviet Union and that it would remain subject to their bullying potential.

The nuclear circle was not confined to the elite five. The domino-effect of nuclear weapons in the hands of the major powers was well reflected in the Third World as the phenomena of insecurity and fear are universal, and state entities' first priority is their redressal. Regional conflicts have proved to be the catalysts in propelling Third World countries to seek the security of nuclear arsenals. India, Pakistan, Israel, Egypt, South Africa, etc. all have had their own justifications of a 'security deficit' that directed them to acquire nuclear weapons. If India decided to have nuclear weapons to meet the China-fear, Pakistan went nuclear due to the India-fear. North Korea and Iran also advance sufficient reasons for such choices as they fear US threats to their regimes. Though the security rationale is not new in the nuclear discourse, the time is now ripe to make a net assessment of the security provided by nuclear weapons, especially when non-state agencies have sufficiently penetrated the state sphere.

An objective analysis of the role nuclear weapons played in the realm of global security entails that, owing to their assumed stabilising effect, no large-scale strategic conflict has taken place during the later half of the 20th century. It is true that we have experienced 65 years of nuclear peace, without the bomb being used in anger. On the other hand, a subjective analysis reveals that stability at the higher level fostered instability at the lower level, known as the "stability-instability paradox." Stability at the nuclear level has provided sufficient space for small scale conventional wars to be fought at the regional level. It is true that since World War II, a global-scale war has not taken place for which nuclear optimists give credit to the effective functioning of deterrence. But many regional wars have been fought for which the theory of deterrence has no convincing answer. North Korea was not deterred from invading South Korea in 1950, nor was North Vietnam from supporting the guerrilla war in South Vietnam in the 1960s. Egypt and Syria were not deterred in 1973 from attacking Israel, or Argentina from seizing the British Falklands in 1982. Neither was Sadam Hussain deterred from seizing Kuwait in 1990 nor was Pakistan deterred for its Kargil plan in 1999.

"What has Changed?"

The British novelist C.P. Snow and British philosopher Bertrand Russell, in the mid-1960s predicted the occurrence of nuclear war "in the next ten years" and opined that unless the nuclear powers drastically reduce their nuclear arsenals, thermonuclear warfare within the decade is a "mathematical certainty." Contrary to their assertions, the world has not yet experienced any such nuclear catastrophe, and we now have that mathematical certainty multiplied by five. However, can we maintain this mathematical certainty for another five decades?

Until now, nuclear weapons have been assigned the role of preventing nuclear war. The logic behind this notion is that there would be total annihilation if a nuclear exchange were to take place; there would be no victor and no vanquished. Throughout these six decades, the devastating power of nuclear weapons has been so vigorously propagated that the world has now learned to live with them, without daring to think of their use in spite of many grave situations. It is now fully established that a nuclear war cannot be won, hence, should not be fought. The contemporary world has been fully reconciled to the symbolic value of nuclear weapons.

But one impending question needs careful examination: should nuclear weapons have any purpose other than preventing a nuclear war? Conventionally, a nuclear weapon has four functions. First, it reinforces a sense of sovereignty and prestige. Second, it provides a tool for intimidation: as a nuclear weapon has a larger audience, the news of its mere possession evokes alarm and respect. The third is deterrence; and the fourth is the use of the nuclear weapon as an instrument of war. All the above functions vindicate only the relation between a state entity and nuclear weapons. Since the end of the Cold War, the nature and nomenclature of the world order in general and the nation-state system in particular have been reconfigured, and also been on constant alternation. There are now competing claims of non-state actors that are rivals to state entities. They have intruded sufficiently into the state sphere, and are here to stay. Does the global nuclear discourse have any room to cope with this changing situation? Is reorientation of the nuclear weapons strategies an imperative now? The areas of concern in locating a convincing answer for these impending questions are given below.

Rival Actors

The world now, in a sense, is bipolar. The so-called sovereign nation states are the prime actors whose malfunctioning or overfunctioning in subsequent stages has given rise to the phenomenon of non-state actors, so also their rivalry. Nuclear discourse, known to be the exclusive domain of state actors, now seems to be a battle ground between them. The fundamental component that makes an entity a legitimate actor is the notion of sovereignty and this sovereignty has been strengthened with the possession of nuclear weapons and the assumed effective functioning of deterrence. Till now, it was thought that illegitimate non-state actors might resort to nuclear weapons owing to their destructive and deterrent power. But the terrorist and separatist organisations may use nuclear weapons as a bargaining chip to claim sovereignty. Al Qaeda can do it, the Liberation Tigers of Tamil Eelam (LTTE) leaders may choose that option. The notion of nuclear weapons as an instrument of war, intimidation, deterrence, and sense of sovereignty is equally attractive to those non-state entities that have imperial designs. Defenders of this apprehension may question the capacity of the terrorist organisations and the chances of the nuclear arsenal slipping into their hands, which has been examined in the subsequent stages of this paper.

New Nuclear Coalition

The revelation of the A.Q. Khan network brought the clandestine nuclear coalition to the surface. The Iran-Pakistan-North Korea nuclear axis can effectively deter external pressure. If powerful terrorist organisations (many were managed by intelligence agencies like the Pakistani Inter-Services Intelligence — ISI — in the past) were to become a part of this coalition, things would be disastrous. The overt or covert backing of other major powers to states that have manipulated the non-proliferation structure in many ways complicates the present nuclear order. If Russia and China were to stay away from Iran and North Korea respectively,the latter's defiance could be pacified amiably. The emerging new coalitions are characterised by both overt and covert nuclear programmes, rooted in nationalistic realism, regional rivalries, political instability, and the willingness to cooperate with other proliferators.

Neo-Deterrence?

The concept of nuclear deterrence is generally designed around state behaviour, and operated in the context of rival military blocs in the past. When non-state actors become forceful entities, the concept of deterrence requires serious reorientation. Again, deterrence is not a panacea. It is also foolish to argue that outbreak of nuclear war would necessarily be a failure of deterrence, and that deterrence was necessarily the sole cause of having avoided a nuclear war. In fact, increased reliance on deterrence has made it difficult to spell out accurately the conditions under which deterrence may or may not work. The argument that "third party deterrence" (delegating deterrence to a state that might aid one's enemies or non-state actors) will be "logical and viable" to counter nuclear threats by terrorists is again a flawed assumption. Terrorist groups thrive under no flag and the votaries of this argument must count the influence of these states on the terrorist groups before delegating deterrence.

The end of the Cold War has not led to the end of the threat of nuclear war. Rather, the nature of the nuclear threat has been changing fundamentally. The nuclear order now seems anarchic and suits the rogue states and non-state actors who are beyond the reach of normal deterrence strategies and diplomacy. Even the no-first-use principle encourages many states to develop their own weapons without fear of nuclear reprisal. The pledge not to use nuclear weapons first would make them even more eager to obtain, and less hesitant to brandish, and use, biological and chemical weapons. Now the Soviet Union is gone. Concepts evolved in a different time, in a different world, are not helpful in perpetuity. A fresh idea is needed. During the Cold War, given the magnitude of the Soviet threat, both broad and focussed deterrence was required. In the new era, we no longer need broad deterrence but the need for sharp deterrence is acute now. Nuclear weapons may be hard to outlaw, but the world can outlive, or outgrow, the nuclear era.

The Report of the Council on Foreign Relations entitled *Preventing Catastrophic Nuclear Terrorism,* by Charles D. Ferguson, asserts that "the probability of nuclear attack has increased because traditional deterrence – threatening assured destruction against a valued asset such as a national territory – does not work against the terrorist groups most likely to covet nuclear weapons."[6] The UN Report of the High-Level Panel on Threats, Challenges and Change, *A More Secure World: Our Shared Responsibility* (2004), enumerates that we live in a world of new and evolving threats where new aspects of the threat – including the rise of a global terrorist network, and the potential for terrorist use of nuclear (biological or chemical) weapons—require new responses because the consequences of allowing latent threats to become manifest, or of allowing existing threats to spread, are simply too severe.

In the post-Cold War world, the threats are regional powers (states) armed with weapons of mass destruction (WMD) long-range delivery mechanisms. In this environment, deterrence is an uncertain tool and capabilities that were formerly stabilising,may now not perform the same function. Theories of nuclear deterrence may not help to deal with "well-protected autocrats imbued with ideals of martyrdom."[7] We need to question the present deterrent role of nuclear weapons and if there is any role at all, then what does this changing role mean in terms of the new global security developments and the new types of weapons under development? While nuclear weapon designs and strategies are under revision and nations are looking at reliable, miniaturised, flexible and credible warheads in the changed world order, a renewed debate on deterrence seems urgently overdue.

For, if a nuclear war is inconceivable, thanks to deterrence strategists, then military doctrines, armed forces development plans and negotiating strategies at arms control talks must change accordingly. The same is true for deterrence strategies. Deterrence should be comprehensive and all encompassing, ensuring the safety, reliability and absolute control of nuclear weapons, fissile materials and mechanisms to deter the non-state actors. It is logical, as Matin Zuberi has emphasised, that nuclear deterrence is no longer the defining principle of the existing nuclear order — rather, it has *moved from the centre to the margin of security policies.* A more anticipatory role is now given to cope with 'rogue' states and terrorist threats (emphasis added).[8]

In this pursuit, Washington's dedicated hunt for national missile defence is an implicit acknowledgement that deterrence, while useful against the Soviet Union during the Cold War, is no longer working against the full spectrum of threats now confronting the US, especially those from rogue states and terrorists.[9] Thomas Reed, former secretary of the US Air Force, in his report, *The Role of Nuclear Weapons in the New World Order* suggested that US nuclear weapons should be targeted at every reasonable adversary around the globe and recommended an option called SIOP ECHO (Standard Integrated Operational Plan, an option for dispatching a nuclear expeditionary force). The US Joint Chiefs of Staff's 1992 Joint Military Net Assessment asserted that nuclear weapons be used to deter not only other nuclear weapons, but also chemical and biological weapons. The logic culminated in the announcement on December 2001 that Washington would formally withdraw from the 1972 Anti-Ballistic Missile (ABM) Treaty in order to pursue missile defences unconstrained by international legal agreements. Also, the Complex 2030 project aims to replace the entire US nuclear arsenal with new "reliable replacement warheads" by the year 2030. The proposed "nukes for ever" project that could cost more than $150 billion over 25 years, is simply a repudiation of the US obligation under the nuclear Non-Proliferation Treaty (NPT) to end the arms race "at an early date" and to negotiate "in good faith" the elimination of its nuclear arsenal.[10]

It is now clear that the United States is moving towards a phase of neo-deterrence with President Bush's farewell to the Cold War deterrence strategy and attempt to bring in a new concept of deterrence in his "Remarks at the National Defense University."[11] Bush noted that today's most urgent threat, unlike in the Cold War era, stems from a small number of missiles "in the hands of these states." Some of "today's tyrants," he said, are gripped by an "impeccable hatred" of the US, its friends, and its institutions. This is why in such a world, Cold War deterrence is "no longer enough," Bush noted.[12] His concept of neo-deterrence, though not drastically different from Cold War deterrence, is based on both offensive and defensive forces, and includes a strategy of counter-proliferation, ballistic missile defence (BMD) and reductions in nuclear warheads. His neo-deterrence framework acknowledges that Russia is no longer the enemy of the US but characterises the world as "still dangerous" with more nations having nuclear weapons and still more having "nuclear aspirations." The US Nuclear Posture Review 2002 appears to have incorporated these and other grave concerns. But a US-driven neo-deterrence framework may not suffice to eradicate the global nuclear menace.

Whether the world can get rid of nuclear weapons and the policy of deterrence that sustains them is difficult to say. It is a truism that nuclear deterrence is a grim but inevitable reality. However, what the present situations warrants is a thorough revision of the concept, aiming to meet the newly emerged challenges. The imperative is a new, global neo-deterrence strategy of active non-proliferation, counter-proliferation and terrorist-proof technology breakthroughs within a new broad cooperative framework specifically to deal with the threat of nuclear technology falling into the hands of non-state actors.

The Fading Nuke Fear

Throughout these six decades, mankind has learnt to adapt to the nuclear environment because nuclear weapons cannot be uninvented. Though we have not forgotten the horrors of the nuclear catastrophe, the thesis of Cold War deterrence has created sufficient trust in favour of the dictum "nuclear war cannot be won, hence, should not be fought." According to Matin Zuberi, "The long period of non-use of nuclear weapons since Nagasaki shrivelled public awareness of the bomb's power to merely a faint apprehension."[13] Though states would continue to have faith in nuclear arsenals as the ultimate source of security, the fear attached to nuclear weapons and their advertent and inadvertent use is gradually fading, thanks to proliferation. In a sense, the traditional deterrence argument has oversimplified the global nuclear dilemma. For example, Iran is now clear that the US cannot afford to initiate a preemptive strike against it if it has its own nuclear bomb. After the Chagai tests, Pakistan is sure that India's conventional superiority has been circumscribed and it cannot dare to resort to a major military operation on the Kashmir issue. In post-Cold War regional conflicts, warfare has been, and will most likely be, confined geographically, and escalation of regional conflicts to global nuclear warfare is not assumed. This assumption lowers the psychological threshold in favour of the actual use of forces, not only for deterrence,but also in regional conflicts.

Growing Nuclear Disillusionment

The effectiveness of the deterrence strategy rests on the resolve to use nuclear arsenals if the situation warrants it. But it has been perceived throughout these six decades that the willingness of the leaders to seriously contemplate use of nuclear weapons has diminished over time.[14] It is true, as argued by Lawrence

Freedman, "that the emperor deterrence may have no clothes, but he is still emperor" but the resolve to nuclear arms reductions is a vindication of the "growing disillusionment" with and "redundancy"of nuclear weapons.[15] With the growing risks regarding the physical protection of nuclear weapons, nuclear deterrence may not be feasible. Further, contrary to popular perception,the large size of the nuclear weapons "decreased rather than increased their attractiveness in the eyes of the professional military."For many, this aspect of these weapons spoiled war for the military.[16]

Fading Nuclear Inhibition

Contrary to the above arguments, the recent trend in nuclear technology innovation reveals that we may yet witness gradual erosion in the global inhibition against the use of 'new' nuclear weapons. The miniaturised nuclear weapons, that nations are planning for would facilitate a "controlled and limited nuclear war." So at the slightest provocation, a small nuke can be used and there may not be any relevance of the deterrence strategy at all. Hence, those who argue that deterrence worked in the past must now ask themselves whether deterrence backed by miniaturised nuclear arsenals would work effectively in the future or not.

Changing Nature of Conflict and Confrontation

The good news in superpower relations did not translate into enhanced regional stability. It appears that the post-Cold War world has ushered in less order and more chaos than previously imagined. Samuel Huntington's *Clash of Civilizations* and Robert D. Kaplan's *The Coming of Anarchy* painted dark visions of a future world caught up in endless conflict and widespread misery.

Owing to the presence of new parameters, a renewed threat assessment for the post-Cold War nuclear warfare is imperative. The global strategic discourse is experiencing a shift in threat from the strategic nuclear attack with global catastrophe as a consequence of the non-strategic ballistic missile attack by 'rogue states' in geographically confined regional conflicts. The Cold War regime assumed 'stability' by way of nuclear deterrence and mutual vulnerability (the so-called mutual assured destruction—MAD) between the symmetrical parties. But the post-Cold War world is marked by instability among asymmetrical parties (i.e. 'rogue states' and non-state actors like international terrorists) who may not follow the logic of deterrence. The pattern of conflicts and confrontation, has transformed from dichotomy to multipolarity and from symmetrical to asymmetrical confrontation, with differentiated actors with different natures.[17] Thus, the post-Cold War security situation is subject to a higher degree of anarchy and unpredictability, with a diffused image of threat. Proliferation of WMD and missile technology worsens this insecurity.

It is hardly expected that the logic of nuclear deterrence will work in post-Cold War regional conflicts due to their complex nature: for example, many actors involved directly or indirectly, or asymmetric confrontation involving various non-state actors such as terrorists. The Cold War nuclear confrontation was basically dichotomous, symmetrical and ideological, and was based on thorough calculations and the rigorous logic of MAD. The United States and Soviet Union shared some values such as the sense of being a superpower and the fear of a global catastrophe which enabled highly technical and rigorous handling to control the situation. However, post-Cold War regional conflicts are fought over the same concrete issues (territory and fundamental values such as religion, ideology)left over by the Cold War, but without a superpower's supervision, thus, are devoid of conviction and remote control. In such a situation,the logic of mutual deterrence could be easily distorted and replaced by human factors such as distrust, revenge, pride, miscalculation and misperceptions.[18]

New Devastating Weapons

A realistic assessment of the capability of today's technology reveals that "conventional weapons delivered by ballistic or cruise missiles could effectively defeat many targets that are usually targeted by nuclear warheads. Precision delivery of nuclear weapons would enable some classes of hard targets to be defeated with much lower yields than are currently employed."[19] Again, the taboo that nuclear weapons are the most dreaded weapons would prove wrong in the future. Though biological and chemical weapons are banned internationally, they are sufficiently devastating and it is wrong to assume that what did not happen in the past, is not likely to happen in the future. Electromagnetic pulse (EMP) weapons and directed energy weapons (DEW) can be effective deterrents for future warfare. There was a time when the destructive capacity of any weapon was measured by the number of people who suffered and the amount of infrastructure destroyed. A nuclear weapon, in that sense, is the highest weapon, having the capacity to destroy the entire earth. The EMP weapons and DEW promise not to kill human beings directly but rather to destroy all communication networks, leading to all civilisation coming to a virtual standstill. They use the electromagnetic spectrum to attack and destroy targets at the speed of light. These are called e-bombs. Digital signal processors, electronic flight controls, telecommunication sets, receivers of electronic warfare (EW) equipment, satellites, HF, VHF, UHF, low band communication equipment, etc are susceptible to the EMP effect. Energy from the explosion of an e-bomb produces high energy electromagnetic pulse – an ultra short, intense microwave – that can effectively destroy electronic systems operating in its frequency range.[20] These weapons are portable and can be dropped by an aircraft over the target. Many countries are now conducting research on this weapon system.

Strategic Uncertainty and Strategic Surprise

The end of the Cold War has led to what may be characterised as an era of strategic uncertainty and strategic surprise. The peace dividend that was expected to accrue after the Cold War, failed to materialise. Instead, numerous small wars and insurgencies broke out all over the world; in a sense, the world order is in a fluid state. The concept of strategic surprise is not new, but the nomenclature of the concept is in the process of disorientation in the post-9/11 era.[21]International literature on strategic surprise mainly relates Pearl Harbour with the attack on the World Trade Centre, unaware of many discernible differences. In the latter case, the enemy is not any particular nation, but a global terrorist network. Furthermore, its targets were primarily civilian, not exclusively military. It did not take public credit for the attack and its goals were not to start or win a war in the traditional sense of the term but to spread terror.

The phenomenon of terrorism is now globalised, so also are its targets. America can be attacked now in Kenya or Tanzania; in other words, any country can be attacked anywhere else.

Threats Within

Many dissent groups within the state may pose sufficient threat to the nuclear weapons and nuclear infrastructure. Though fabricating and/or pilfering a full-fledged nuclear bomb is difficult for them, sabotaging a nuclear facility by a suicide attack or by using a 'dirty bomb' is undoubtedly within their reach. One discernible change in the targeting strategies of these dissent groups is that now they target civilians more than the government establishment, only to inflict widespread terror. Even their accessibility to sophisticated technology is very high. To that extent, their linkage with the global terror network is well established. In their mission, nuclear weapons or materials would be lucrative as their ramifications are perilous. It would be easy for these dissent groups to spread terror far and wide through the nuclear route, as public perception on anything nuclear is blurred.

Changing Nature of Terrorism

It may be argued that threats to nuclear weapons are not new; even nuclear terrorism as a phenomenon is as old as the history of the proliferation of nuclear technology itself. However, the post-Cold War- post-9/11 world is very different from the previous era. Equally, there is a perceptible change in the *modus operandi* of terrorism itself. A study on the recent trends in terrorism explains the changes in the type, number, and lethality of terrorist attacks, the attitudes of terrorist groups, infrastructure such as that related to command and control, capabilities, recruiting, and financing, etc. The 2006 State Department Report on trends in terrorism identified that there is increased sophistication in all terrorist operations The nature of modern terrorism is that anyone can be a victim, but terrorism is not random. Now, a growing percentage of terrorist attacks are designed to kill as many people as possible. In the 1990s, a terrorist incident was almost [20] per cent more likely to result in death or injury than an incident two decades earlier. The trend toward higher casualties reflects, in part, the changing motivation of today's terrorists.

If we look at the number of terrorist incidents and number of casualties during the last three decades, it is quite clear that terrorism can occur in any form. Instances of international terrorist incidents during 1980-84 numbered 2,500, while casualties during the same period numbered 6,500. But during the period 1994-99, the number of terrorist incidents was 2,000 but the number of casualties had risen phenomenally to 18,000.[22] This reveals that despite a general decrease in the numbers of terrorist incidents over these years, there is a strong trend toward greater number of casualties. The US National Counter-Terrorism Centre reported in 2005 that roughly 40,000 individuals were wounded or killed in terrorist incidents as compared to 9,300 the previous year and 4,271 in 2003. Reported terror-related deaths in 2005 numbered 14,602 as compared to 1,907 deaths in 2004, and 625 in 2003.[23] The report placed the number of total reported terrorist attacks in 2005 at 11,111 as compared to 3,168 in 2004 and 208 in 2003. Out of the 11,111 attacks reported, 6,000 or roughly 54 per cent, were against facilities and resulted in no casualties. If this trend continues, it is more likely that terrorists would resort to the nuclear route as it can cause greater casualties than any other method.

II

Security of Nuclear Weapons

Conventional wisdom on nuclear weapons as purely security assets deserves a second thought in the post-9/11 era. No doubt, the end of the Cold War has dramatically reduced the risk of nuclear war, but the legacy of the nuclear danger continues in many other forms, posing serious challenges to international security. The major challenge is the likelihood of nuclear technology slipping into the hands of terrorists, and its consequent misuse. Thomas Kean, the chairman of the 9/11 Commission, therefore, rightly, said, "A nuclear weapon in the hands of a terrorist is the single greatest threat ... today."[24] Former US Energy Secretary Bill Richardson also voices his apprehension on the misuse of nuclear technology, saying that "in the 20th century, nuclear deterrence worked. In the 21st century, it won't. MAD deterred the Soviet Union, but nothing will stop suicidal *jihadists* from using a nuclear bomb if they get their hands on one."[25] Also, it is quite clear by now that most of the threats of the 21st century emanate not from states but from societies – from social trends and fault lines. Does today's nuclear discourse adequately address the societal linkage of nuclear threats?

The nuclear weapon, as perceived to be playing the security-provider role, may no longer be able do so, as its own security is at stake now. If this is so, the post-9/11 era is bound to undergo a transition from the era of "security by nuclear" to "security of nuclear." A few perceptible changes in the relation between the nation-state and nuclear weapons vindicate this transition. Firstly, the non-state actors and their willingness and capability to acquire nuclear weapons would effectively challenge the nation-state's monopoly over nuclear weapons. Secondly, in the extreme, in the case of a nuclear catastrophe caused by a non-state entity, a nation-state would become defenceless, thus, raising obvious questions on its 'sovereignty'. Thirdly, the concept of deterrence that worked effectively between the superpowers during the Cold War would fail to operate in the case of terrorists as they have no address to be attacked in retaliation. If this is so, the global nuclear order would become anarchic, given the gravity of the risk of nuclear technology falling into the hands of terrorists, and the resultant consequences.

Secrecy is considered the best security for nuclear weapons. But the strategy of deterrence based on MAD has made the nuclear discourse democratic and overt to give an impression to the adversary that it has the will and capability to retaliate in equal degree. In other words, the balance of nuclear terror gives stability. But the terror potential of nuclear weapons is equally lucrative for illegitimate actors to achieve their objectives far better. The following section examines the chances of nuclear terrorism that seems to be the major source of threat to nuclear weapons, which nuclear optimists consider the ultimate source of security for nation-states.

The Phenomenon of Nuclear Terrorism

Nuclear terrorism as a phenomenon is not new; it had captured the public's imagination way back in the 1970s. The best-selling international spy thriller, *The Fifth Horseman,* in which Libya's Muammar Gaddafi tries to force the US to support the Palestinian cause by threatening to blow up New York City, brought the phenomenon into public domain. The nightmare scenario of a 'nuclear winter' – how the world would slowly die in the aftermath of a nuclear war – in the movie, terrified the public. Coupled with imaginary thoughts, the stray attempts by some extremist groups to acquire nuclear materials to build the bomb during the 1990s brought the issue into the global strategic discourse. The disintegration of Soviet Russia and the uncertainty over its scattered nuclear materials, facilities and personnel made the apprehension deeper. With the demolition of the twin towers of the World Trade Centre, the phenomenon of nuclear terrorism came centre-stage as the incident showed a trailer on the capability, motivation and resolve of a terrorist group to unleash unacceptable damage on its target.

In general, the apprehension of "increasing probability of terrorists using radiological weapons"[26] mainly emanates from the negative popular perception regarding anything nuclear, the projected reach of the terrorists, and the vocabulary of 'nuclear terrorism' itself. As the magnitude of the threat of nuclear terrorism is unknown yet and such a precedent is unavailable, this apprehension is bound to emerge. But a realistic assessment of different facets of nuclear terrorism – accessibility of the required materials, affordability of the terrorist entities – entails that the feasibility of such an incident at the micro level seems more probable than a nuclear attack at the macro level.

The phenomenon of nuclear terrorism is "neither a single entity nor a narrow category."[27] It encompasses a broad spectrum, from low level incidents of threats involving radioactive material through attacks on reactors to a detonation of a full-fledged terrorist nuclear bomb.[28] It could also range from spreading a small amount of radioactive material by different means to the use of a large powerful weapon misappropriated from the state arsenal. Other terminologies used for nuclear terrorism are radiological terrorism, super terrorism, hyper terrorism, high-tech terrorism, etc. Broadly, nuclear terrorism can be classified under two heads:

(I) Low Probability with High Consequence: Terrorism Using Nuclear Weapons/Materials

- Fabrication of a nuclear device by terrorists on availing all the required means and materials through the black market or state sponsorship.
- Theft or misappropriation of a nuclear device from a state arsenal and detonation of the same.
- Detonation of a radiological dispersal device (RDD) or an improvised nuclear device (IND).

(II) High Probability with Low Consequence: Terrorism Using Non-Nuclear Strikes on Nuclear Installations/Facilities

- Attack or sabotage of a nuclear reactor or facility, leading to environmental contamination by the release of radiation.
- Sabotage of fuel storage or other nuclear facility.
- Damage to spent fuel storage pool.
- A widely publicised nuclear threat that proves to be a hoax.

The beginning of any form of nuclear terrorism is the terrorists' access to radioactive materials, without which there can be virtually no nuclear terrorism. Their access to radioactive materials may be possible in many ways: the most common path is illicit trafficking, state sponsorship, obtaining unauthorised assistance from the senior officials of the establishment, assistance from custodians of nuclear materials, or by seizure. The chances of access to nuclear devices are greater when a nuclear capable country undergoes political unrest. Thus, terrorists have broadly five ways to carry out their objectives:[29]

1. Theft and detonation of an intact nuclear arsenal.
2. Theft, purchase or trafficking of fissile materials leading to the fabrication and detonation of a nuclear weapon.
3. Sabotage of a nuclear facility, power plant, research laboratory or medical facility where radioactive sources are used.
4. Fabrication of a 'dirty bomb' – RDD or radiation emission device (RED)— by unauthorised acquisition of industrial or medical radiation sources.

5. A widely publicised probable nuclear attack that later proves to be a hoax, but the negative popular perception on almost anything nuclear is sufficient to create havoc in society.

Among these five forms, the first two are horrific forms of nuclear terrorism or macro-level nuclear terrorism that would inflict horrendous damage to life, property and the environment. The third and fourth types are considered as low level of terrorism that probably would cause less damage, hence, can be categorised as micro-level nuclear terrorism. There is an agreement among the experts that nuclear terror with the highest consequences is the least likely to occur owing to the difficulty in its accomplishment, and acts with the least damaging consequences are the most likely to take place as they are relatively easy to carry out.[30] The fifth type of nuclear terrorism we are almost experiencing and there is now widespread concern across the globe on the issue.

'Why' of Nuclear Terrorism

Before knowing the 'how' of nuclear terrorism, it is pertinent to understand the 'why' of the phenomenon first. The nuclear weapon has both terrorised and fascinated humankind. *"Fear of the bomb"*, says Joseph Cirincione, the vice president for national security at the Centre for American Progress, "motivated the first atomic programme; the *allure of the bomb's* power later propelled national leaders to build ever-larger arsenals. Today, fear of a nuclear attack by terrorists ... has made nuclear proliferation the number one security threat ...."[31] (emphasis added). This *fear and allure* inherent in the nuclear bomb are equally attractive for the terrorists. The other side of the 'why' is that there is a phenomenal rise of terrorist organisations and also their capability. Also, a clear-cut distinction can be traced in the nature of terrorism in the pre- and post-Cold War periods. The paradox of the post-Cold War period is the substantial growth of terrorism perpetrated by many groups that cannot be pigeon-holed into any clear-cut category such as nationalist-separatist, left-wing, right-wing, religious terrorist group, etc. Though many terrorist groups in the past threatened to resort to the nuclear path, they could not overcome their conservativeness regarding tactics and level of violence in the pursuit of their goals. But the newer terrorist groups in the post-Cold War period are more violent, more innovative, and more willing to use mass-killing weapons.[32] Thus, the answer to the question 'why' terrorists might resort to nuclear weapons lies in some of the following assertions:

1. *Deterring Deterrence:* While a state possessing nuclear weapons can effectively deter its adversary, it cannot deter a non-state actor since he doesn't have a return address. But a terrorist organisation possessing a nuclear arsenal can bring a state to its knees. The nuclear weapon could be an effective deterrent for the terrorist organisations against coercive state action. With the possession of the ultimate weapon, a terrorist outfit can effectively blackmail a state and bargain for its cause from the ultimate platform of strength.
2. *Manipulating Negative Societal Perception:* Nuclear terrorism has the feature of achieving a unique type of public fear and trauma because of the negative societal association for almost anything nuclear. The public's irrational fear of radiation can well be exploited by the terrorists.
3. *Unique Identity:* The prestige and unique identity factor involved in the possession of nuclear power would instigate a terrorist organisation to acquire it. By acquiring nuclear capability, a terrorist outfit could assume a quasi-state nature. That would separate the entity from other entities since the mere identity of 'being nuclear' would certainly ensure that it had vast coercive power, with the ability to have considerable impact on the public and government.
4. *Proportionate Value:* The popular fear of nuclear weapons and the panic involved with such an act exactly matches the aims and objectives of terrorism. The nuclear weapon today is a highly feared weapon and mere possession by any sub-state actor would serve its purpose to the maximum.
5. *Enduring Impact:* Of all weapons, only a nuclear detonation would guarantee immediate massive destruction. Also, the resultant impact would continue. Even the mere news of its possession by terrorists would create uncontrollable mass disruption.

'Who' of Nuclear Terrorism

Like the varied forms of nuclear terrorism, there are also many groups that might resort to the nuclear path. Charles D. Ferguson and William C. Potter have broadly categorised them into the following four groups: [33]

1. Apocalyptic Groups.
2. Politico-Religious Groups.
3. Nationalist/Separatist Groups.
4. Single Issue Terrorists.

The apocalyptic group believes in purifying the world via violent upheaval and the use of the nuclear weapon would be the best option to accomplish their objective. The politico-religious groups have come to dominate the post-9/11 phenomenon of terrorism. These groups range from the broad network of Al Qaeda to the more geographically focussed Hezbollah, Lashkar-e-Tayyeba, and the Hindu fundamental extremist groups which are hybrids of both political and religious motivations.[34] The nationalist/separatist groups include organisations whose purpose is to achieve some political objectives on the basis of their ethnic, regional or separate identity. The LTTE in Sri Lanka, the Kurds in Turkey, the Irish Republican Army in Ireland, etc. are some such outfits that might consider the inflicting of harm on their oppressors through nuclear means, and to force state authorities to concede to their demands. The single-issue terrorist category includes the animal liberation activists, anti-abortion advocates, pro-environmentalist groups, and the anti-nuclear activists who may, in a remote chance, resort to nuclear terrorism. From all of the above, the groups that more likely to resort to nuclear terrorism are the politico-religious groups and the nationalist-separatist groups.

The discourse on terrorism in general does not end with the technical-resource dynamics of any terrorist outfit. Nuclear terrorism, in particular, is closely linked with terrorists' psychology and motivation. All terrorists have a theoretical ability to cause mass casualties but resorting to the nuclear path is rooted in the psycho-dynamics of the group, rather than in any single terrorist's choice.[35] The popular belief that terrorists are psychopathic or psychotic, sick, crazy, etc. is misleading. Resorting to terrorism is not an aberration. Most terrorists are psychologically normal and as rational as anyone else and they do not reveal major psychopathology. So, their strategy and decision to resort to the nuclear path would be well calculated. "A possible motivation for nuclear terrorism would be the group's belief that it has nothing to lose."[36] Since every terrorist group's core priority is its survival, it would give good thought before being resorting to the nuclear path because the post-attack actions by the concerned state and international community may completely wipe out the outfit. However, a group might resort to nuclear terrorism to regain its status when it is about to be dissolved or its survival is at stake – a terrorist's "Samson Option" or the Biblical situation of David and Goliath. It might also go nuclear to prevail over, or become more prominent than, other groups. Another psychological aspect of it is that "terrorists are technologically conservative" and probably that's why there is no instance where terrorists have resorted to nuclear weapons.[37] They prefer to use tried and tested methods to achieve their aims; they don't follow the trial and error method since the chance of success in their every such operation is fifty-fifty.

'How' of Nuclear Terrorism

As stated earlier, there is no precedent of nuclear terrorism till date and it may not occur in the future also. Even a thorough scrutiny of the necessary conditions for nuclear terror to take place reveals that the threat of nuclear terrorism is overstated, and popular wisdom is flawed. However, no conclusion can be drawn on terrorism, and nuclear terrorism, if it takes place, would be the worst incident ever to happen to mankind. The following section examines all probable forms of nuclear terrorism and their chances of occurrence. On the basis of empirical evidences, literature and the assertion of the technical personnel, this paper takes the position that the chances of macro-nuclear terrorism are remote owing to the technical difficulties involved, but an incident of nuclear terror at the micro-level seems not impossible.

Theft and Detonation of an Intact Nuclear Weapon

The first form of nuclear terror i.e. theft and detonation of an intact nuclear weapon, necessitates a terrorist group with an extreme objective to acquire the necessary technical and financial resources for carrying out such an operation. It must prepare a blueprint of how to bypass or defeat safeguards in and around the nuclear weapons reserve. Then the appropriated device must be transported to a high-value target for detonation. So the route to successful action of the plan is very long, thus, the chances of the long chain being severed are high, and the plan could easily be thwarted at many points, if it is leaked or detected.

State Sponsorship

A (rogue) state might deliberately transfer, sell or share nuclear weapons with a terrorist group but such a combination is a 'worst case scenario'. Prior to 9/11 (January 2001), the US Department of Defence concluded that "the likelihood of a state sponsor providing such a weapon to a terrorist group is believed to be low."[38] Potential cases are Pakistan, North Korea, Iran and such other "rogue states." The apprehension is that leaders supportive of radical Islamist groups may come to power in these countries and transfer an intact nuclear weapon to their patron terrorist organisation. Chances of such transfer are high during a coup or at a time of extreme political unrest. Although the chances of possible loss of control over nuclear arsenals cannot altogether be refuted, all regimes can be expected to regard nuclear weapons as crucial symbols of power and to employ the most reliable military or state security forces to guard them. Though the chances of loss of nuclear weapons are high during and after political instability, "the elite security forces are most likely to perform their protective duties."[39] If the coup is successful, the new regime will have the same drive as its predecessors to guard its nuclear arsenal.

Defying Security Arrangement

Nuclear weapons generally are kept under tight security during their entire life cycle, including production, transit, storage, and deployment. This system has a number of mutually reinforcing components like personnel reliability programmes to verify the loyalty and emotional stability of custodians, physical protection measures (barriers, alarms, controlled access arrangements, armed guards, and response forces), careful weapon accounting practices, the principle of the requirement of more than one individual to gain access, and other measures to prevent unauthorised use. Even if terrorists get access to, or acquire, an intact nuclear bomb, the in-built security system with the bomb would be difficult for them to penetrate. Most countries now use the permissive action link (PAL) system, designed to ensure maximum security of their warheads. The PAL is an electronic locking system with multiple six or twelve-digit codes integrated into the warhead's design. These locks allow only a limited number of attempts to enter the correct codes: if the limit is exceeded, circuits in the arming mechanism self-destruct or disable the warhead.[40] Weapons are also safeguarded against unauthorised use through safing, arming, fusing, and firing (SAFF) procedures. For instance, the arming sequence for a warhead is generally designed to ensure that the warhead can be used only according to a specific mission profile, not for all missions in general. Finally, weapons are also protected from unauthorised use by a combination of complex procedural arrangements and authenticating codes authorising each individual to activate the weapon.[41]

Acquisition of Radioactive Materials and Knowhow

The second argument on the possibility of occurence of nuclear terrorism is the fabrication of a nuclear bomb by terrorists accessing the required materials, knowhow and technical support. This apprehension has been strengthened with the revelation of the A.Q. Khan network. Though the chance of state sponsorship is remote, the officials and security personnel in charge of the radiological materials and the bomb may succumb to the temptation to facilitate the illicit transfer to the terrorists. Through trafficking channels, the terrorists can get the required radiological materials and hire technical personnel to fabricate their own bomb. Two types of fissile material could be used for making the bomb – highly enriched uranium (HEU) and plutonium. These materials have been produced in great quantity in the nuclear weapon and civilian nuclear energy programmes around the world. Russia has access to more than 34 metric tonnes of weapons-usable materials annually and there is an equal amount in the United States.[42] According to the International Atomic Energy Agency (IAEA) about 25 kg of HEU or 8 kg of plutonium would be needed to manufacture a first-generation weapon.[43]

However, getting hold of the required radioactive material, technology and knowhow is not easy for the terrorists. Nuclear materials or weapons are considered national treasures and are provided lifetime security in every country. Though the number of cases of illicit trafficking has been on the rise in recent years, the quantity of weapon-usable radiological material trafficked is not much. Out of 662 confirmed incidents of illicit trafficking in the past 12 years, there have been 18 confirmed incidents involving HEU and plutonium.[44] The data reported to the IEAE Illicit Trafficking Database (ITDB) in 1993–2004 shows a long-term downward trend in the occurrence of incidents involving nuclear materials. Though the ITDB recorded a substantial increase in the number of such incidents from 2000 to 2004, none involved HEU or plutonium which are necessary for making the bomb.[45]

During the 1990s, with the collapse of the Soviet Union and consequent political instability, the chances of theft of radiological materials from its poorly guarded scattered facilities were acute. Though there were some reports on the alleged sales of radiological materials by the unpaid workers,[46] most of these attempts were thwarted. Now the Russian facilities have been secured and both Russia and the US are cooperating to secure all the scattered materials and facilities of the former Soviet Union.[47] Officials of the 12th Main Directorate of the Ministry of Defence, responsible for the security and safety of Russia's nuclear weapons, have repeatedly stated that Russia's arsenal is secure from terrorists.[48]

Even if the terrorists get access to radiological materials, it is impossible for them to have the infrastructure and extremely complex technology required to produce sufficient quantities of weapon-usable materials. Even if the terrorists manage to get HEU, they cannot use it directly since HEU is generally available in the form of uranium hexafluoride or oxide. It needs to be processed into a form usable in a nuclear device — an act that involves technical complexity and huge resources.

Worldwide stockpiles of HEU are plentiful at about 1,850 metric tonnes, enough to make tens of thousands of nuclear weapons.[49] A major chunk of this is under military control. Like enriching uranium, making plutonium without state sponsorship, is beyond the capability of the terrorists. No doubt, since

1999, global stocks of plutonium have increased but HEU stocks are declining.[50] Again, the highly radioactive spent fuel is not easy to be acquired by terrorist groups if they don't have access to the "special handling gear." Thus, it is clear that though fissile materials may be theoretically accessible to terrorists, the required resources and expertise to utilise them for fabricating a device are not easily available.

Sabotage of a Nuclear Facility

The above discussed forms of terrorism, one way or the other, do not appear feasible. But one of the conceivable ways of nuclear terrorism is the sabotage of a nuclear facility, power plant, laboratory or medical facility by terrorists that could lead to a nuclear explosion and release of radiation. Various techniques might be employed by terrorists in this regard, ranging from the launching of a rocket, mortar, throwing of a grenade to crashing of an airplane. The event of 9/11 has strengthened this apprehension. Such an action would inflict large scale psychological stress and social disruption, radioactive contamination, and financial damage, but not a large number of deaths.

Not only commercial power plants, but also research reactors, are potential terrorist targets. About 280 of these reactors are operating in 36 countries.[51] Internationally, there is no binding mandate that states must meet minimum security standards at research reactors or commercial power plants. Though the IAEA has issued voluntary guidelines which have been widely adopted, these are very broad and lack specificity. Spent fuel storage facilities are potential terrorist targets. Most countries store spent fuel within the boundary of the nuclear reactor site. More than 200,000 metric tonnes of such spent fuel have been accumulated worldwide.[52] The consequence of a successful terrorist attack on a spent fuel storage site could create a radioactive disaster by the dispersion of radiation. Waterborne attack is another form of nuclear terrorism. Every nuclear plant requires some means of supplying external cooling water. Generally, power plants are accessible by the sea, a lake, or a river. A terrorist can reach the reactor site through the water channel and sabotage it. Terrorists can also disturb the vital water supply channel and attempt to block the water flow that would eventually lead to disturbances in the functioning of the reactor.

Research facilities, medical establishments, food processing units, etc., using radiological materials are also vulnerable to terrorist attacks. Though the amount of radiological material used is little, the level of security is uneven in these facilities. Nearly 100 civilian facilities around the globe operate with small amounts of weapon-grade HEU (uranium enriched up to 90 per cent or more). Commercial radioactive sources are used in virtually every nation in various applications such as cancer treatment, industrial radiography, oil well logging, and scientific research laboratories. In numerous medical centres, radiological materials like Cobalt 60 are used for treatment of cancer__ these are virtually outside any national security structure. These facilities are the soft targets of the terrorists for spreading radiation. The same is the case of food processing units where radiological materials are used for preserving and processing food items. Though the damage or radiation contamination level would be less compared to an attack on a nuclear reactor or the detonation of a bomb, its psychological effect would be far greater.

Dirty Bomb

Another possible tactic of the terrorists to tap into the general public fear is to explode a conventional explosive coupled with radioactive material, known as the "dirty bomb". Whatever amount of radioactive material is accessible to the terrorists would be sufficient to fabricate a radiological dispersal device (RDD) which is much easier to make than an improvised nuclear device (IND). The RDD is a very simple device. It is a mixture of conventional explosive with radiological material, for example, TNT (trinitrotoluene) packaged with radioactive material. If an explosion takes place, the radioactive material will spread in a sort of dust cloud carried by wind which will reach far away places. Cobalt 60, Cesium-137, Iridium-192, and Strontium-90 isotopes are RDD usable weak nuclear materials generally trafficked internationally and the conventional explosives are already easily accessible to the terrorists.[53]

Unlike the radioactive materials, terrorists wouldn't have much trouble getting their hands on high explosives. Dynamite is readily available, and TNT is not too hard to come by. The main limitation in fabricating the dirty bomb would be the availability of radioactive material, which is not nearly as accessible as explosive material, but there are a number of sources for radioactive material around the world. For example:

- Hospitals use small quantities of radioactive material such as Cesium-137, in nuclear medicine. Cancer treatment institutes use Cobalt-60 for radiotherapy of cancer.
- Universities use similar materials to conduct scientific research.
- Food irradiation plants use radiation from Cobalt-60 to kill harmful bacteria on food.
- Natural radioactive uranium isotopes are mined for use in nuclear energy. Terrorists could conceivably acquire uranium from various mines.
- There are a number of abandoned "nuclear batteries" scattered around the former Soviet Union. These portable thermoelectric generators contain a sizeable amount of Strontium-90, a highly potent radioactive isotope.
- Terrorists can collect spent radioactive fuel from Russian reactors, which have been abandoned in old nuclear submarines, among other places.
- They can also put something together using various low-level radioactive materials that are easily available.[54]

Precedents

The phenomenon of nuclear terrorism on a large scale seems a remote possibility. But spreading of radiation through various other means is not impossible. We cannot be certain that a terrorist incident of a high level will not take place. Though there is no such precedent available, there are records of attempts by different groups to acquire the necessary technology or materials. One such instance of a terrorist group attempting to build its own nuclear weapon was the Japanese group Aum Shinrikyo that tapped into its vast financial resources to buy Australian properties and conducted an investigation for purchasing uranium-enrichment technologies.[55] But it failed, largely because enrichment is an extremely challenging process, requiring state-level resources. Such other attempts[56] by different groups are:

- In 1987, thieves stole a large radiotherapy source from a disused hospital in Goiana, Brazil.

- In November 1995, Cesium-137 was discovered in a Moscow park.
- In December 1998, RDD was found near Argun, Chechnya.
- Multiple attempts by Al Qaeda to acquire material for a radiological device.
- UK intelligence – Al Qaeda prioritised RDD from 1999 onwards.
- Jose Padilla, arrested in May 2002, was reportedly planning to develop uranium-based RDD, and targeting of apartment blocks using conventional weapons.
- Murder of Alexander Litvinenko in London in November 2006, by Polonium-210 ingestion
- A Briton, Dhiren Barot, was sentenced to life imprisionment in 2006, for planning to build a "dirty bomb" out of some 10,000 smoke detectors, each of which contained a small radioactive source.

III

Measures So Far

The quality of regulatory and physical security arrangements across the globe is highly variable. Even developed countries face difficulties in securing their radioactive materials. In the United States, with comparatively strong and sophisticated security arrangements, it is estimated that every day one radioactive source becomes orphaned by theft or abandonment.[57] The accountancy and control of these materials in the developing world are known to be much weaker. Although with increasing international awareness, national regulations have been tightened in some countries, they remain lax in many others.

Hence, one can assume that nuclear terrorism is a fact waiting to happen. The world cannot enjoy the comfort of unavailability of a nuclear terror precedent. Across the globe now there is concern for the security of radiological materials. At least, the fear of a possible nuclear terror catastrophe has raised the awareness of the world to locate and deal with such possible cases. The US is now working with more than 70 countries in this respect. A recent multilateral initiative in this regard was the UN Security Council Resolution 1540 that criminalises the proliferation of WMD, including nuclear weapons. The resolution calls upon all states (1) to promote the universal adoption of multilateral treaties whose aim is to prevent proliferation of WMD; (2) to adopt national rules and regulations by preparing a national control list, where it has not yet been done, to ensure compliance with their commitments under the key multilateral non-proliferation treaties. The resolution calls upon states to develop and maintain effective measures for accounting, securing, and physically protecting these items, as well as effective border controls and law enforcement efforts and effective national export and trans-shipment controls.[58]

The second important multilateral initiative was the adoption of an international convention addressing the threat of nuclear terrorism by the UN General Assembly on April 13, 2005. The treaty also makes the possession, use, or threat of use of radioactive devices by non-state actors, their accomplices and organisers a criminal offence.[59] The convention urges states to ensure the protection of radioactive materials by formulating national laws on the lines of the recommendations of the IAEA. It classifies any attempt or attack on a nuclear facility, which could risk the release of radioactive material, as a punishable offence. The convention also obliges governments to either prosecute terrorist suspects or extradite them to their home countries. It further encourages sharing of information and greater cooperation between countries.

Bilateral partnerships are also being built for reducing the chances of terrorists' access to nuclear arsenals. In the immediate post-Cold War period, the Nunn-Lugar Act (1991) attempted a cooperative threat reduction programme to provide assistance for dismantling, safe storing and establishing verifiable proliferation safeguards of the weapons in the Soviet nuclear arsenals. The latest initiative is the Global Initiative to Combat Nuclear Terrorism (GICNT) launched by US President George W. Bush and Russian President Vladimir Putin on July 15, 2006, with the aim "to prevent the acquisition, transport, or use by terrorists of nuclear materials and radioactive substances or improvised explosive devices using such materials, as well as hostile actions against nuclear facilities."[60] Two other US programmes are already in operation to prevent the transfer of radiological materials to terrorists. The Material Protection, Control and Accounting (MPC&A) Programme of the US Department of Energy (DoE) provide equipment and training to upgrade security at existing sites of the Russian Federal Agency of Atomic Energy housing fissile materials.[61] The US Department of Defence (DoD) programme to construct the Mayak Fissile Material Storage Facility intends to provide a highly secure location for plutonium and HEU taken from dismantled Russian nuclear weapons.[62] The DoE also manages the Russian Surplus Fissile Materials Disposition Programme, commonly known as the Plutonium Disposition Programme to facilitate implementation of the September 2000 Plutonium Disposition Management and Disposition Agreement under which Russia and the US will each dispose of 35 tonnes of excess weapons-grade plutonium by immobilisation or utilisation in MOX fuel.[63] The US National Nuclear Security Administration (NNSA) is providing training to officials from other countries on procedures to account for, and control, nuclear material, and physical protection measures for critical nuclear sites.[64] By the end of 2008, efforts to improve nuclear security through the US-Russian Bratsilava Initiative will be near fruition.

Other broad based programmes include the Proliferation Security Initiative (PSI) and the Container Security Initiative (CSI). In 2003, the PSI was launched to promote international cooperation to interdict WMD-related shipments and to cutoff the channels of proliferation finance. More than 70 nations are now cooperating to prevent the proliferation of WMD materials. No doubt, efforts to counter nuclear terrorism are growing in size and scope, but many more serious efforts are needed to prevent illegal transfer of nuclear material and knowhow.

Conclusion

Nuclear terrorism in the post-1990s, specifically in the post-9/11 era, is a conceivable phenomenon for two reasons: one, because of the easy availability of fissile material or micro-proliferation ; second, because of the changing nature of the political, psychological and organisational characteristics of terrorism itself. So the very nature of the terrorist behaviour is at the core of the problem. As there are no precedents except for a few unsuccessful attempts, one cannot draw a definite conclusion on this subject. As of now, the only terrorist entity that has the presumed capability to resort to the nuclear path is Al Qaeda. Documents found in Afghanistan reveal that while Al Qaeda's efforts to make nuclear weapons may be far less sophisticated than known state programmes, it seems it is determined to get them and willing to use them.[65]

One report says that the idea of attacks on nuclear power stations by Al Qaeda was raised in the early stages of the planning of the 9/11 attacks, but was vetoed, apparently by Bin Laden himself.[66] But assuming that Al Qaeda is not going down the nuclear path is also erroneous. Except in a few cases, the behaviour of terrorist groups cannot be predicted. They may not use the nuclear weapon but mere possession of a nuclear device by them is sufficient to create havoc.

It is a truism that the invention of nuclear weapons has given rise to completely novel conditions that have fundamentally altered the concept of war in contemporary human history. They were first used not as war-fighting but "war-ending assets." During the Cold War, nuclear weapons were considered as "weapons of deterrence" and in the post-Cold War world order, if the strategies and use of nuclear weapons are not redefined, they would prove to be *"weapons of burden."* As nuclear weapons are here to stay, it would be prudent not to bureaucratically extend the concept of deterrence to the prevailing world order, and find comfort in the thought that a nuclear arsenal would take care of our security as well as its own.

Notes

1. Stephen J. Cimbala, "Nuclear Weapons in the New World Order," *The Journal of Strategic Studies*, vol. 16, no. 2, June 1993, p.184.
2. Scott D. Sagan, "Why Do States Build Nuclear Weapons? Three Models in Search of a Bomb," *International Security*, vol 21, no. 3, Winter 1996-97, pp. 54-86). Also see David Krieger, "Why Nations Go Nuclear," URL: http://www.wagingpeace.org/articles/2005/11/00_krieger-why-nations-go-nuclear.htm
3. MemCon, January 26, 1956, *Foreign Relations of the United States, 1955-1957* (Washington D.C.: US Government Printing Office) vol. 20, p. 297.
4. Scott D. Sagan and Kenneth Waltz, *The Spread of Nuclear Weapons: A Debate* (W.W. Norton, 1995).
5. "Groves to Stimson," July 18, 1945, Truman Library (Internet), quoted in Gerard J. Degroot, *The Bomb: A History of Hell on Earth* (London: Pimlico, 2005), p. 62.
6. Charles D. Ferguson, "Probability of a Nuclear Attack by Terrorists Has Increased, Warns Council Report," *Council on Foreign Relations*, March 28, 2006.
7. Matin Zuberi, "Relevance of Nuclear Deterrence in the post-Cold War Era," in *The*

Relevance of Nuclear Deterrence, Delhi Policy Group, Nuclear Policy Stewardship Project, 2006, pp. 32-33.

8. Zuberi, Ibid., p.35
9. Mitchell B. Reiss, "The Nuclear Tipping Point: Prospects for a World of Many Nuclear Weapons States," in Kurt M. Campbell et al. ed., *The Nuclear Tipping Point: Why States Reconsider Their Nuclear Choices* (New Delhi: Manas Publications, 2005), p. 11.
10. Jacqueline Cabasso, Complex 2030: US Plans for "Nukes Forever", Executive Director, Western States Legal Foundation, available at:www.wslfweb.org/docs/2030cabasso.pdf
11. George W. Bush, "Remarks at the National Defense University," Washington D.C., May 1, 2001, Washington D.C.: US National Archives and Records Administration, *Weekly Compilation of Presidential Documents,* vol. 37, no. 46, pp. 1652-1658.
12. Bush, Ibid., pp. 686-687.
13. Zuberi, n.7.
14. Henry Kissinger, "We need Star Wars," *Washington Post,* Outlook Section, September 8, 1958.
15. Jack N. Barkenbus, "Devaluing Nuclear Weapons," *Science, Technology, & Human Values,* vol. 14, no. 4, Autumn 1989, p. 426.
16. Barkenbus, Ibid., p. 429.
17. Masako Ikegami, "Missile Defence and Nuclear Deterrence in Post-Cold War Regional Conflicts," Stockholm University, URL: http://www.isodarco.it/courses/candriai03/paper/candriai03-Ikegami.pdf
18. Ikegami, Ibid.
19. Stephen M. Younger, "Nuclear Weapons in the Twenty-First Century," Los Alamos National Laboratory, June 27, 2000, URL: http://www.fas.org/nuke/guide/usa/doctrine/doe.younger.htm
20. "High Power Microwave (HPM)/E-Bomb," URL: http://www.globalsecurity.org/military/systems/munitions/hpm.htm
21. Charles S. Parker, Eric K Stern, *Political Psychology,* vol 23, no. 3, September 2002, pp. 601-630.
22. "Terrorism Becoming More Dangerous," URL: http://www.fas.org/irp/threat/p5.gif
23. Raphael Perl, "Trends in Terrorism: 2006," CRS Report for Congress, July 21, 2006, Congressional Research Service, Library of Congress.
24. Quoted in Charles B. Curtis, "Promoting Global Best Practices," Institute for Nuclear

Materials Management 46th Annual Meeting, July 11, 2005, p.2, URL: http://www.nti.org

25. Bill Richardson, "Preventing a Nuclear 9-11," URL: http://www.richardsonforpresident.com, March 28, 2007, accessed on March 29, 2007.
26. The US National Security Strategy for Combating Terrorism (February 2003) warned that "the probability of a terrorist organization using a chemical, biological, radiological or nuclear weapon or high yield explosives has increased significantly during the past decade" and consequently within a few weeks of 9/11, President Bush ordered his national security team to give nuclear terrorism priority over every other threat to the US. For details, see *National Strategy for Combating Terrorism,* February 2003, URL:http://www.whitehouse.gov/news/releases/2003/02/counter_terrorism/counter_terrorism_strategy.pdf
27. Robin M. Frost, *Nuclear Terrorism After 9/11,* Adelphi Paper 378 (New York: Routledge, 2005), p. 11.
28. Gavin Cameron, *Nuclear Terrorism: A Threat Assessment for the 21st Century* (London: Macmillan Press Ltd., 1999), p. 1.
29. For different forms of nuclear terrorism, see Charles D. Ferguson and William C. Potter, *The Four Faces of Nuclear Terrorism* (New York: Routledge, 2005).
30. Mathew Bunn and George Bunn, "Strengthening Nuclear Security Against Post-September 11 Threats of Theft and Sabotage," *JNMM,* Spring 2002, pp. 48–60 and "Nuclear and Radiological Threats", Chapter 2 of Committee on Science and Technology for Countering Terrorism, National Research Council, *Making the Nation Safer: The Role of Science and Technology in Countering Terrorism* (Washington, D.C.: National Academy Press, 2002).
31. Joseph Cirincione, *Bomb Scare: The History & Future of Nuclear Weapons* (New York: Columbia University Press, 2007), p. xi.
32. "Terrorism: Motivations and Causes," URL: http://www.terrorism.com/modules.php?op=modload&name=News&file=article&sid=5693&mode=thread
33. Quoted in Ferguson and Potter, n.29, pp. 18-20.
34. Ferguson and Potter, Ibid., pp. 18–19.
35. Frost, n. 27, p. 41 and Cameron, n. 28, p. 135.
36. Cameron, Ibid., p. 135.
37. Ibid., pp. 135-136.

38. US Department of Defence, *Proliferation: Threat and Response* (Washington: Government Printing Office, 2001), p. 62.
39. Ferguson and Potter, n.29, p. 60.
40. Peter Stein and Peter Feaver, *Assuring Control of Nuclear Weapons*, CSIA Occasional Paper # 2, Centre for Science and International Affairs (Harvard University, 1987).
41. Gurmeet Kanwal, "Comand and Control of Nuclear Weapons in India," *Strategic Analysis*, January 23, 2000.
42. Statement of Linton F. Brooks before the 108th Congress House Armed Services Committee, March 4, 2003, www.globalsecurity.org/wmd/library/congress/2003_h/03-03-04brooks.htm
43. Kalpana Chittaranjan, "The IAEA as a Safeguards Regime," URL: http://www.nuclearfiles.org/menu/key-issues/nuclear-energy/history/article-chittaranjan-kalpana.htm
44. "Nuclear Trafficking Latest Statistics Released," Staff Report, September 27, 2005, URL: http://www.iaea.org/NewsCenter/News/2005/traffickingstats.html
45. "Illicit Nuclear Trafficking: Facts & Figures," URL: http://www.iaea.org/NewsCenter/Features/RadSources/Fact_Figures2004.html
46. For details on Russian activities, see "The Human Factor and Security Culture: Challenges to Safeguarding Fissile Materials in Russia," Preliminary Report, November 2002, Centre for International Trade and Security, University of Georgia, USA, URL: http://www.uga.edu/cits/documents/pdf/Humanfactor.pdf.
47. Kenneth N. Luongo, "The Uncertain Future of US-Russian Cooperative Security," *Arms Control Today*, January/February 2001.
48. See, for example, statements by Gen. Igor Valynkin, *Interfax*, September 4, 2002.
49. Mohamed El Baradei and Jonas Gahr Støre, "How the World Can Combat Nuclear Terrorism," Disarmament Documentation, Acronym Institute, URL:http://www.acronym.org.uk/docs/index.htm
50. Charles D. Ferguson and William C. Potter, "Improvised Nuclear Devices and Nuclear Terrorism," URL: http://www.wmdcommission.org/files/No2.pdf.
51. *Nuclear Power in the World Today*, Nuclear Issues Briefing Paper 7, February 2005, URL: http://www.uic.com.au/nip07.htm
52. George Bonn, Fritz Stenhausler, and Lyudmila Jaitseva, "Strengthening Nuclear Security Against Terrorists and Thieves Through Better Training," *The Non-*

Proliferation Review, Fall/Winter 2000, URL: http://cns.miis.edu/pubs/npr/vol08/83/83bunn.pdf.

53. Robin Frost, "Nuclear Terrorism Post 9/11: Assessing the Risks", URL: http://www.cda-cdai.ca/symposia/2003/frost.htm
54. Frost, Ibid.
55. For details, see "The Demand for Black Market Fissile Material," URL: http://www.nti.org/e_research/cnwm/threat/demand.asp
56. "Nuclear Terrorism", URL: www.comm.cornell.edu/als481/Nuclear.ppt
57. Ferguson and Potter, n.29, p. 291.
58. S/RES/1540 (2004), April 28, 2004. URL: http://daccess-ods.un.org/access.nsf/Get?Open&DS=S/RES/1540%20(2004)&Lang=E&Area=UNDOC
59. International Convention for the Suppression of Acts of Nuclear Terrorism, URL: http://www.un.int/usa/a-59-766.pdf
60. "UK Joins Global Initiative to Combat Nuclear Terrorism", URL: http://www.irna.ir/en/news/view/menu-234/0608011297165947.htm
61. "Plan for Securing the Nuclear Weapons, Material, and Expertise of the States of the Former Soviet Union," URL: http://www.carnegieendowment.org/pdf/npp/Nuke%20Security%20Report%202-5-3%20(1).pdf
62. "178 STC 05 E-The Security of WMD Related Material In Russia," URL: http://www.nato-pa.int/default.asp?SHORTCUT=695
63. S.G. Cochran et al., "Fissile Material Disposition Program Final Immobilization Form Assessment and Recommendation," October 3, 1997, Lawrence Livermore National Laboratory, URL: http://www.osti.gov/bridge/servlets/purl/605164bSbqmb/webviewable/605164.pdf.
64. Jacquelyn S. Porth, "Efforts to Counter Nuclear Terrorism Grow in Size and Scope," URL: http://media-newswire.com/release_1045979.html
65. David Albright, *Al Qaida's Nuclear Programme: Through the Window of Seized Documents,* Nautilus Institute Special Forum 47, November 6, 2002, URL: www.nautilus.org/fora/special-Policy-Forum/47_Albright.html#sect2
66. *The 9/11 Commission Report: Final Report of the National Commission on Terrorist Attacks Upon the United States,* Official Government Edition (Washington, DC: US Government Printing Office, 2004), URL: http://www.gpoasccess.gov/911/pdf/full-report.pdf, p. 172.

2

Nuclear Terrorism and India's Preparedness

Assessing Probability, Weighing Strength and Identifying Weakness

"Nuclear terrorism is the top fear for Americans," says a survey conducted recently by the California-based Saga Foundation.[1] About 74 per cent of the focus groups surveyed believe that a terrorist strike within the US is imminent and 40 per cent of them are of the view that the attack will involve a nuclear device. Also, nearly 50 per cent Americans fear Al Qaeda acquiring nuclear weapons more than they fear other nuclear weapons and rogue states. If the citizens of the sole superpower have such apprehensions, how afraid should the Indians be when New Delhi is surrounded by unstable nations with WMDs and the dominant presence of many non-state entities in the subcontinent?

India harbours a sizeable atomic infrastructure scattered across the country. The phenomenon of terrorism is also ubiquitous in the country. But a plausible conjunction of the two – 'nuclear terrorism' – is surprisingly not publicly debated, firstly, because of the notion that such a precedent is unavailable, whereby it is assumed that such an incident would not take place. Secondly, it is also believed that the nuclear installations in India are comparatively safe – under strict civilian control, with an adequate security blanket. Thirdly, until 1998, the entire attention of the strategic community was concentrated on the country's nuclear weapon status and its inhibitions to cross the Rubicon. More contemporarily, the issue of India's energy security and the role of nuclear energy in its energy mix have dominated the strategic discourse. Lastly, following the 'culture of secrecy', the scientific-political leadership is extra cautious to avoid unnecessary public panic as the popular perception on anything radioactive is blurred; therefore, they prefer not to publicise the issue or even publicity assess India's preparedness to face such a situation. However, the Indian nuclear establishment is confident of its emergency preparedness, the strength and structure of its nuclear facilities and opine that "the regulatory infrastructure currently in place is adequate" to face any eventuality.[2]

This chapter is an endeavour to assess the risk of nuclear terrorism in India, the vulnerabilities of nuclear facilities and India's preparedness to face such incidents, if they ever were to take place. The chapter undertakes a theoretical appraisal of possible threats to Indian nuclear facilities and then assesses their probability. Though it is difficult to fathom the exact risks, probabilities and consequences of such an incident, this study examines the general trend of terrorism in and around the subcontinent, the geographical distribution of nuclear facilities vis-à-vis the existence of terrorist belts, motivation and operational capabilities of various terrorist/extremist groups in this part of the region. Finally, an assessment is made of the security arrangements in and around nuclear facilities, the mechanisms at state disposal to monitor and respond, the existing legal framework to arrest any slippage of nuclear materials and knowhow into the wrong hands. The chapter concludes with a prescriptive note to further strengthen these efforts.

Real Concerns or False Alarms?

During the past few years, nuclear security seems to have overshadowed the political agenda in many parts of the world as also in India. Concern on a probable nuclear terror incident in the country has gradually started to draw the attention of the political leadership and the scientific community and this development is a result of four consequent happenings. Firstly, the global debate on nuclear terrorism, especially in the post-9/11 period, has markedly been reflected upon the Indian national security discourse. Secondly, the evolving Indo-US strategic relationship has led to the fear of threat from Al Qaeda because anybody who is seen as a friend of the US becomes its target. Thirdly, political instability in Pakistan and fear of its nuclear arsenal falling into the hands of extremist-terrorist groups has equally attracted attention.

Fourthly, the apprehension regarding probable nuclear terror is further consolidated, based on the increasing reported incidents of smuggling of fissile material in India and in the region as a whole.

A series of intelligence reports have revealed that terrorists could target India's nuclear infrastructure. These threats and possible security breaches have led the Indian government to reorganise and enhance security at vital civilian nuclear installations throughout the country. On the eve of Independence Day, 2006, security was stepped up at India's premier nuclear organisation, the Bhabha Atomic Research Centre (BARC), with deployment of the elite National Security Guards (NSG) for the first time, following inputs of a possible terrorist attack.[3] In addition to the BARC's own security system, the Central Industrial Security Force (CISF), Mumbai Police, NSG and army personnel were posted inside BARC. The NSG was deployed in view of the gravity of the threat, while the CISF was deployed in place of the State Reserve Police from June 1, 2006. In September 2006, National Security Adviser M.K. Narayanan claimed that the security structure of nuclear establishments had been completely revamped and the "arrangements are adequate for the threats we face ..." [4]

While inaugurating a three-day conference of state police chiefs in New Delhi on November 22, 2006, India's Home Minister Shivraj Patil said that the proposed civil nuclear deal with the US has made the country's atomic power plants and other critical infrastructure "highly vulnerable" to terrorist threats.[5] The main among the suspected plotters, he said,was the Lashkar-e-Tayyeba (LeT). Fears were heightened over the possibility of the LeT infiltrating a nuclear plant when reportedly three Muslim men were arrested for entering the Narora nuclear power plant with fake IDs in August 2006.[6] Later in the same month, local residents reported seeing two armed men breaching security at the Kakarapar nuclear power complex near Surat.[7] The event prompted a massive security force response that included the deployment of commandos throughout sensitive areas of the complex. In August 2003, three radioactive isotopes of Cobalt-60 were reportedly stolen from the tightly guarded Tata Iron and Steel Company (TISCO) in Jamshedpur.[8] These apprehensions got further consolidated with the news that a uranium based ash analyser had been stolen from the Coal Mines Planning and Designing India Limited (CMPDIL) Complex in Ranchi, Jharkhand, in December 2006.[9] The analyser contained 300 milli curie uranium. The Hazaribagh police set up a team to trace the analyser.[10]

Much before these incidents, there were some reports on smuggling of radiological material into India. In July 1998, the Central Bureau of Investgation (CBI) was reported to have unearthed a uranium theft racket when it seized 6 kg of uranium, and arrested two persons.[11] Later, it reportedly seized 2 kg more, as well as a 31 kg piece of plutonium, and arrested another person. In 1998, BBC brought out a report on the arrest of a politician, Maheswar Singh Deo, in West Bengal who was allegedly carrying "more than 100 kilograms of unrefined uranium."[12] Indian intelligence officials suspected that the politician was part of a group smuggling unrefined uranium to neighbouring Pakistan.[13] Another incident of uranium smuggling, reported by BBC, was unearthed in 2001, when police arrested two men with more than 200 grams of semi-processed uranium in West Bengal.[14] Police sources said the uranium was being smuggled into Bangladesh from the Jaduguda uranium mines in Bihar.

Stories of uranium smuggling, in both Indian and international media, are not new. Especially, uranium smuggling from the Jaduguda mines was mentioned in the US government reports dating as early as the 1970s. An Office of Technology Assessment Report to the US Congress, dated June 1977, mentioned that:

> In April 1974, a uranium smuggling operation was uncovered in India. All of the details of the incident are not available, but it appears from the rather sketchy press accounts that uranium was being removed from the Jaduguda plant in Bihar [now Jharkhand], India, and was being smuggled to Nepal. From Nepal, it was smuggled to Hong Kong where reportedly Chinese or Pakistani agents took delivery. It is believed that as much as $2.5 million worth of uranium may have been involved.[15]

More recent reports dealing with the international dimension of illicit trafficking in nuclear and radioactive materials have also pointed out that uranium ore stolen from the Jaduguda mines found its way into Nepal, headed for the international black market.[16] Another report, authored in the fall of 2004 on nuclear trafficking routes, detailing trends in Southern Asia, offers the following information: "In 2001, smuggled uranium, confiscated from suspected terrorists in Balurghat, northern West Bengal, had been removed from the Jaduguda uranium mines in Bihar [now Jharkhand] and was planned to be smuggled across the Bangladeshi border."[17]

However, before drawing any alarmist conclusion from the above data, a few things need to be kept in mind:

(i) Most of the above information is compiled from newspaper/website reports. These can be taken as being only of limited credibility. In the absence of any authoritative estimates and reports, it would be difficult and imprudent to reach any hasty conclusions.

(ii) The amount of material smuggled is very small and unrefined, therefore, hardly sufficient to make any explosive device to cause nuclear terrorism.

(iii) Reports are indicative of the existence of a nuclear and drug-trafficking route in Southern Asia. In fact, the South and Southeast Asian regions have seen illicit nuclear proliferation and radioactive material smuggling that has affected many countries.[18] This is hardly surprising given that South Asia, particularly India, is situated between the two well-established drug trafficking routes – the Golden Crescent and Golden Triangle.The Golden Crescent which constitutes Asia's principal area of illicit opium production, is located at the crossroads of Central, South and Western Asia, overlapping three nations: Afghanistan, Iran, and Pakistan. The Golden Triangle is Asia's main opium-producing area constituting around 350,000 sq km that overlaps the mountains of three countries of mainland Southeast Asia: Myanmar, Laos and Thailand. It has been marked that radiological smuggling follows this traditional route.[19]

Map 1
Drug Trafficking Complex

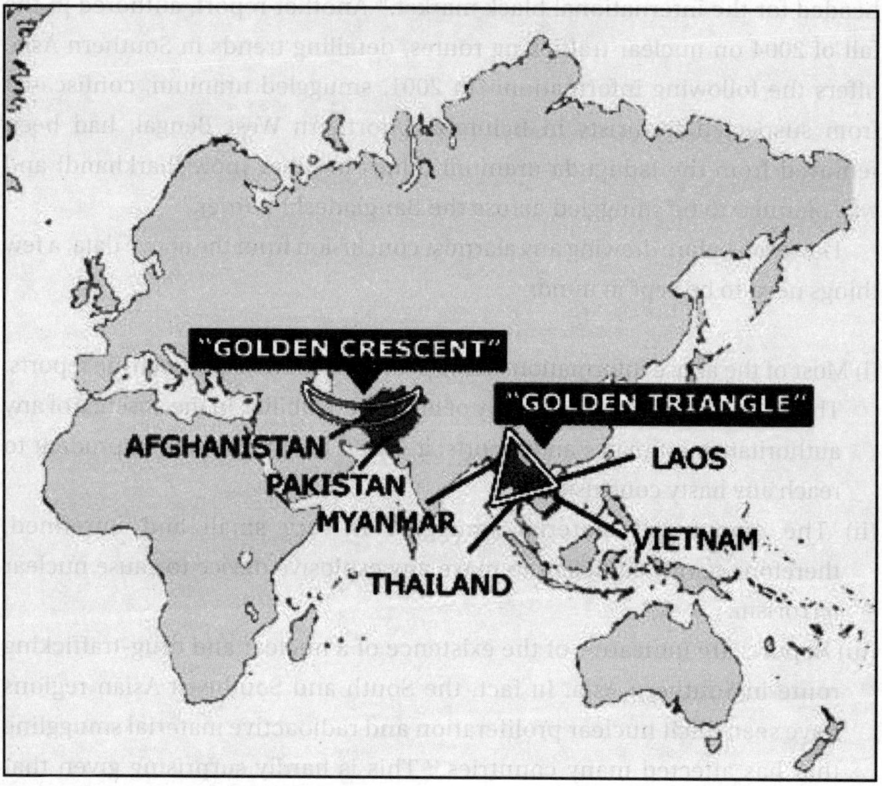

Source: http://upload.wikimedia.org

Besides the traditional trafficking and smuggling routes, the recently revealed Proliferation Wal-Mart in Asia led by Pakistani nuclear scientist A.Q. Khan which is conducted with the knowledge of the Pakistan government[20] vindicates the fact that a nuclear black market did, and can, flourish in or from Asia.

Security Structure in Indian Nuclear Establishments

The Indian nuclear establishment, comprising a range of activities, is spread across the country. As shown in Map 2, in the extreme north, Nangal (Punjab) has a heavy water facility; in the northeast is the Domiasat uranium mine; in the east, the

Talcher heavy water plant; in the extreme south, the Kudankulam reactor facility; and in the west, there is situated a constellation of facilities in the states of Maharastra, Gujarat, Kerala and Karnataka. In central India, nuclear power plants are located in the state of Uttar Pradesh and in the southeast part of Rajasthan.

Map 2

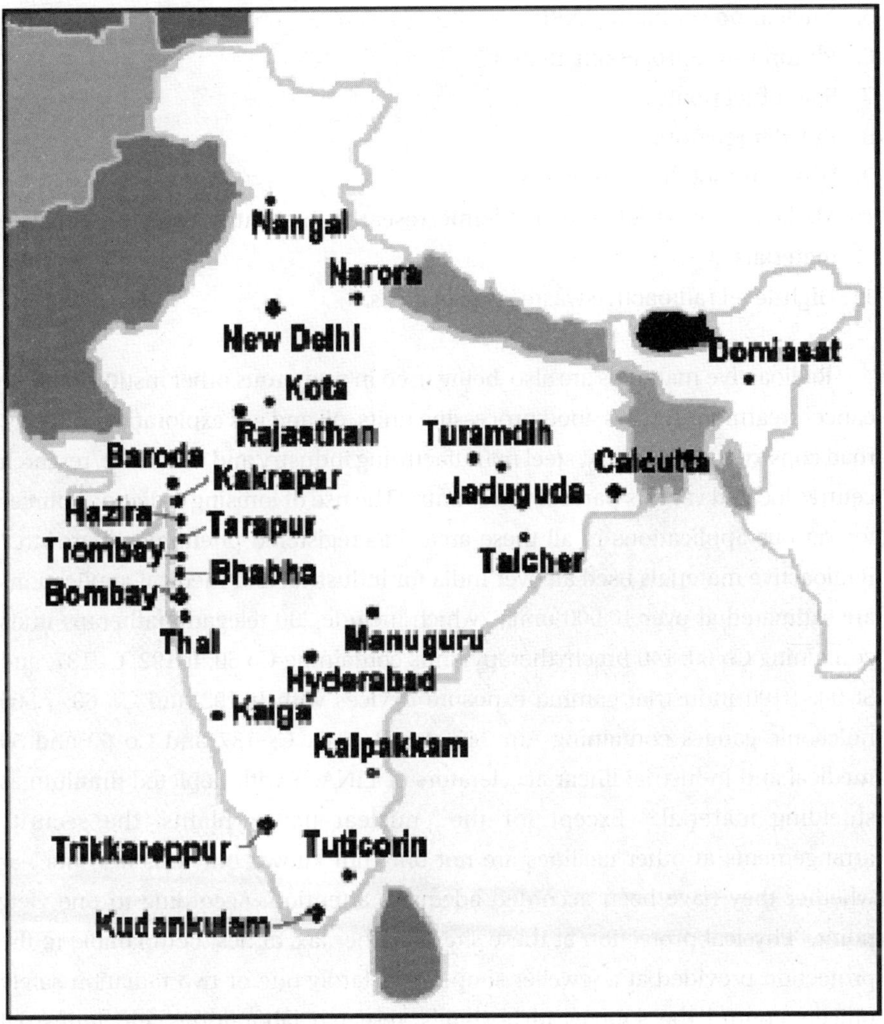

Source: http://images.google.co.in

The Indian nuclear facilities scattered across the geographical spread of the country mainly comprise:

1. Uranium/thorium mines and milling plants.
2. Transport network of nuclear materials.
3. Fuel fabrication facilities.
4. Research reactors.
5. Nuclear power plants (NPP).
6. Plutonium reprocessing plants.
7. Spent fuel pools.
8. Breeder reactors.
9. Waste immobilisation plants.
10. Medical, industrial and academic/research institutes using radioactive materials.
11. High-level radioactive waste storage areas.

Radioactive materials are also being used in numerous other institutions like cancer treatment centres, food processing units, oil and gas exploration industry, road construction industry, steel manufacturing industry and academic/research centres located various parts of the country. The use of ionising radiation sources for various applications in all these areas has registered phenomenal growth.[21] Radioactive materials used all over India for industrial and medical applications are estimated at over 10,000 units[22] which include 230 telegammatherapy units containing Co 60; 140 brachytherapy units containing Co 60, Ir 192, Cs 137, and Sr 90; 1,100 industrial gamma exposure devices with Ir 192 and Co 60; 7,500 nulceonic gauges containing Am 241, Am-Be 241, Cs 137 and Co 60 and 50 medical and industrial linear accelerators or LINACS with depleted uranium as shielding material.[23] Except for the nuclear power plants, the security arrangements at other facilities are not only not known but it is also unclear whether they have been accorded adequate attention. According to one view point, "Physical protection at these sites is rather lax, at best comparable to the protection provided at a jeweller shop… ."[24] Hardly one or two radiation safety officers control the sources in hospitals, research laboratories and industrial plants.[25] Even detailed information on the structure and quality of security arrangements in place for the Indian nuclear reactors is not in the public domain.

For instance, few know that there are different levels of security rings around every power plant. All the facilities are surrounded by physical barriers aiming to restrict easy access to sensitive areas. Access control is maintained over personnel by visually verifying laminated identity cards.[26] The CISF, a central government paramilitary security force, is responsible for protecting nuclear installations in the country. In addition, each facility has its own security personnel. Every facility is surrounded by two fences – inner and outer – having a double-layer security structure. The distance of the outer fence is about 1.5 km (sterilised zone) from the inner fence (exclusion zone), therefore, even if an intruder manages to penetrate the outer security ring, it would be extremely difficult for him to break through the inner security circle as the second layer of security is even tighter, and is deployed with sophisticated surveillance systems.[27] A graphical structure of the security arrangements around the facility is presented below (Fig. 1).

Fig. 1

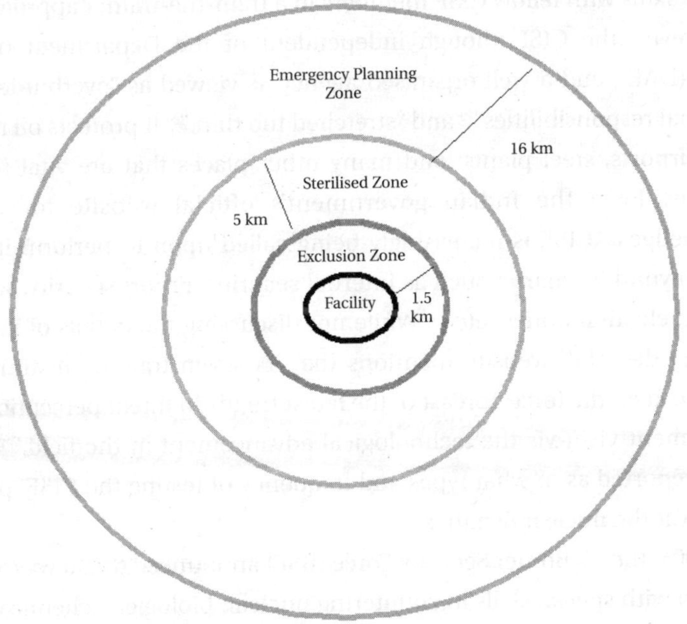

In the sterilised zone, which expands up to 5 km, habitation is restricted. In the emergency planning zone that expands up to 16 km, though there is no restriction on population settlements, and constant monitoring is undertaken for security and emergency planning purposes. A close watch is kept over transportation networks, means of communication, etc. Considering the advanced means of communication and transport facilities available now, intruders can stay outside the security circles but traverse the distance easily to enter at an appropriate time. Therefore, it may be prudent to put in place another security ring covering a larger area, perhaps of a minimum of 50 km radius, around the facility.

The CISF is developing the necessary ability to deploy specially-trained first responders in case of a nuclear attack. Four companies of the CISF have been sanctioned, and specialised training is being imparted to some 400 personnel. This elite force is deployed in four locations across the country: Ghaziabad unit to cater to Delhi and other northern areas, Ranchi unit to cater to the eastern areas, Kota unit for the western areas, and Chennai unit for the southern part. Many officers of these units have already undergone eight weeks of nuclear and biological response training in the United States, and others are being trained to share skills with fellow CISF members in a train-the-trainer approach.[28]

However, the CISF, though independent of the Department of Atomic Energy (DAE), and a well organised agency, is viewed as "overburdened with additional responsibilities"[29] and "stretched too thin."[30] It protects oil refineries, ports, airports, steel plants, and many other places that are vital for India's economy. Even the Indian government's official website for the CISF acknowledges, "CISF is increasingly being called upon to perform important duties beyond its charter such as internal security, airport security, security of highway, election duties, etc."[31] While not discussing the details of its training methods, the CISF website mentions that its seven training institutions are trying "to keep the force abreast of the latest trends in threat perception and its management vis-à-vis the technological advancement in the field."[32] It is not openly reported as to what types and frequency of testing the CISF personnel undergo at the nuclear facilities.

In 2004, India's Border Security Force (BSF) announced that it was forming a battalion with special skills in countering nuclear, biological, chemical threats.

The special battalion will receive training from nuclear experts at BARC. In April 2002, the chairman of India's Nuclear Power Corporation announced that he was cognisant of the terrorist threat and mentioned that the DAE and CISF have performed security drills at nuclear facilities. The Indo-US Working Group on Counter-Terrorism has discussed a variety of issues, including nuclear terrorism. The United States has reportedly brought up the issue of assistance to secure Indian nuclear facilities. But such assistance faces the accusation of India becoming subservient to the US. The IAEA has provided security training for the Indian officials. Also, Indian experts have participated in the IAEA-sponsored International Training Course on the Physical Protection of Nuclear Facilities and Materials operated by the Sandia National Laboratories.[33]

The safety and security of a facility mainly depend on four factors: (1) adequate number of guards; (2) comprehensive training of these guards; (3) strict monitoring, warning systems, disaster management arrangements; and (3) proper personnel reliability procedures. No doubt, the number of security personnel deployed in the nuclear power plants (NPPs) must be adequate but increasing the number of guards in the facilities does not necessarily increase the safety of the facilities. More guards, in fact, could increase the threat from insiders. If newly hired guards are not thoroughly screened, saboteurs could infiltrate the facility. Even if the new guards are well screened, screening procedures are not foolproof, and a rapid increase in new employees increases the probability of some malicious people being admitted.

The DAE appears to have attended to all the above four aspects. However, considering India's ambitious plan to expand its nuclear establishment, it is necessary be wary to avoid complacency. While increasing the number of guards might appear to increase security, certain countervailing human behaviour might actually weaken security if only the number of guards is increased. The authorities may convince themselves that they are recruiting loyal employees, but "organisations that pride themselves on high degrees of personnel loyalty can be biased against accurately assessing and even discussing the risk of insider threats and unauthorised acts." After an employee clears a background check, he could become the target of coercion and blackmail by terrorists. A strict implementation and periodical assessment of an advanced personnel reliability programme is the need of the hour. Also, it is crucial to undertake a thorough assessment of the design basis threat (DBT) of all Indian nuclear facilitates in the light of Al Qaeda's growing influence. Besides the external physical security in place, the inbuilt safety mechanisms in the nuclear installations assume greater importance where the inside-sabotage factor is concerned.

Facets of Nuclear Terrorism in India

There is no precedent of nuclear terrorism yet. Nor have any of the terrorist outfits or extremist entities, operating in and around India, overtly shown any interest in resorting to the nuclear path. Al Qaeda is known to have contacted A.Q. Khan, and documents recovered from Afghanistan show that Osama bin Laden was initially considering the designing of a nuclear explosive device, but later gave it up. The reasons may be that it is too difficult to materialise such a design owing to the requirement of sophisticated technology and expertise. Also, it may be assumed that terrorist entities may be preparing for such a plan, but have not yet achieved the required capabilities. But considering the way terrorism has spread to every nook and corner of the country and the sporadic instances of smuggling of small quantities of radioactive materials, if the terrorists were to get hold of the required capabilities, it could be the beginning of a nuclear terror plan. It could be expected that the terrorist outfits operating in India or in the subcontinent would have the basic knowledge of Indian security arrangements, vulnerable areas and topography. In this context, it would be prudent to think about the kinds of nuclear terrorism (as identified in the first chapter) that could take place in India and the types of entities that might resort to such acts. Broadly, nuclear terrorism is of two types: (1) terrorism using nuclear weapons/materials which is of low probability, but high consequences; (2) terrorism using non-nuclear strikes on nuclear installations/facilities whose occurrence is more probable but would have lower consequences.

A most plausible scenario of nuclear terrorism in India would be the misappropriation of a small radioactive source (irrespective of all the difficulties) of about nine grams (10,000 curies) of Co-60 from a cancer radiotherapy unit and dispersed by five pounds of TNT. This would contaminate an area of about two sq km, or about 33 city blocks, to a level that would require clean-up.[34] If this kind of incident takes place in Delhi, depending upon the location of detonation and direction of the wind, it would immediately affect Connaught Place, India Gate, South and North Block, Darya Ganj, etc. Since Delhi is the political heart of India, the possible impact on the political life of the country would be severe. Even if such an extreme situation does not take place, false news of a nuclear terror incident would create massive disruption, throwing life in a city like Delhi into chaos. Such a hoax would raise a false alarm among the public, causing many road accidents and horrible traffic jams. The entire Ring Road of Delhi would be choked, entry to, and exit out of, the city would be difficult, many patients on their way to hospitals would die, rescue operations would be difficult, and normal life would be disrupted. The same would be the case with Mumbai or any other metro in India.

Even a small amount of HEU, which is odourless, kept in a crowded place, subway of a city, market or railway station would cause radiation without being detected as radiation detection devices are not widely used in India except in the nuclear facilities, airports and other sensitive areas. A dirty bomb may not be a weapon of mass destruction but "its disturbing consequences qualify it as a weapon of mass disruption." In any such incident, "Public hysteria would overwhelm local authorities, the economic consequences would be long lasting, and government agencies responsible for public safety would come under severe scrutiny."[35]

Adnan Gill, a Pakistani columnist,in a report titled "How secure is the Indian nuclear programme?" in *The Pakistan Tribune,* on October 17, 2006, branded the security standards in place for the Indian nuclear programme as "primitive and outdated at best."[36] He has identified the following five scenarios wherein a well conceived attack on Indian nuclear assets by any number of highly-motivated insurgents and/or their sympathisers can potentially materialise:

Scenario 1: The insurgents steal an intact nuclear weapon from BARC and detonate it in the middle of Mumbai.

Scenario 2: The insurgents fashion a crude nuclear weapon by stealing fissile material from the Kalpakkam Atomic Reprocessing Plant (KARP) and explode it in Chennai.

Scenario 3: The insurgent sympathisers smuggle highly radioactive material out of the nuclear fuel complex to detonate a radiological dispersion device or 'dirty bomb' in Hyderabad.

Scenario 4: Naxalites sabotage the KARP facility to cause large release of radiation in Chennai.

Scenario 5: In the aftermath of a massive tsunami, insurgents effortlessly get their hands on unguarded nuclear weapons stored at the unsecured military bases and fissile materials from the KARP, BARC and/or Tarapur Atomic Power Stations and disperse these weapons and fissile materials all over India. They also sell the loot, and stage multiple nuclear attacks.

Gill's assertion, however, does not stand up to scrutiny. First, India's nuclear arsenals are known to be in a disassembled state.[37] Also, the inbuilt security structure with the warhead – a multi-layered electronic locking system which, at each stage, requires the code to make it functional – is extremely difficult to penetrate. Even if the terrorists manage to acquire some fissile materials, it would be impossible for them to fabricate a complete bomb as fashioning such a bomb requires state-level resources. His fourth assertion that Naxalites may sabotage facilities in Chennai is again fallacious on the ground that the Naxalites would not go to the extent of sabotaging a nuclear facility owing to the fact that their operations would be affected in the area. It would have been of some value if Gill had considered the LTTE as a potential threat to the nuclear facilities in Tamil Nadu. Also, his information on the devastation of KARP, BARC and Tarapur facilities by a tsunami and Koodankulam by an earthquake is abysmally wrong as nothing serious or of the magnitude he is depicting has ever happend. Rather this proves that Indian facilities can withstand such eventualities.

However, this doesn't mean that the Indian nuclear establishment is completely secure from the menace of terrorism. It can be targeted in many ways and is also vulnerable to many eventualities. Broadly, these can be categorised under the following heads:

1. Threats from terrorists operating inside the country: Jaish-e-Mohammad (JeM), Lashkar-e-Tayyeba(LeT), Harkat-ul-Mujahideen(HuM), etc.
2. Threats from terrorists operating outside the country, but with sufficient presence and links with the groups operating inside: Al Qaeda, LTTE, etc.

3. Vandalism by politico-religious groups: Rashtriya Swayamsevak Sangh (RSS), Vishwa Hindu Parishad (VHP), Shiv Sena, Hindu or Muslim fanatic groups, other extremist religious groups
4. Acts by nationalist/separatist groups: Kashmiri separatist groups, Naga insurgents, Naxalites, etc.
5. State sponsored terrorism from across the border.
6. Destruction by natural disasters and nuclear accidents owing to human or technical errors: tsunami, cyclone, earthquake, etc. when terrorists can take advantage of the vulnerability.

Therefore, the forms of threats that the Indian nuclear establishments may experience are broadly three:

(a) Threats from outsiders.

(b) Threats from insiders.

(c) Threats from the forces of nature.

As a corollary to the first point, a threat to a nuclear facility in a neighbouring country is also a strong threat to India as most of the neighbouring countries are politically unstable. Chances of illegal transfers to the wrong hands are high.

Given the geographical spread and location of the facilities, religious-chauvinistic factors, socio-politico-administrative issues, national rivalries and possibilities and consequences of natural disasters, the terrorist threats to Indian nuclear establishment could occur in the following forms:

1. **Aerial Attacks:** As a result of air bombings,unmanned aerial vehicles (UAVs) attacks, aircraft crashing into a nuclear plant, rocket launching.
2. **Land Attacks:** Throwing hand grenades, truck bombs, suicide attacks, commando attacks, theft of radioactive materials, and detonation (dirty bombs), attacks on the transportation vehicle containing radioactive materials, etc.
3. **Sea Route Attacks**: Attack by the enemy from the sea route as most of the facilities are located near the sea; terrorists can enter the facility by a boat containing explosive and explode it near the facility.
4. **Damage by Natural Disasters:** Tsunamis, cyclones and earthquakes that throw security arrangements at nuclear facilities into disarray, leading to possible leakage of unguarded material.

5. **Nuclear Hoax:** Exploitation of negative public perception of anything nuclear, thereby, causing havoc in the society.
6. **Cyber Attacks:** Hacking into computer systems or unleashing computer works or viruses to strike at India's nuclear infrastructure.

Assessing the Capability and Motivation of the Terrorists

Though terrorism is a major challenge before India and modern day terrorists intelligently leverage communication and financial networks, the probability of a nuclear terror incident may be determined by factors like (1) location of nuclear facilities (source of the radioactive material); (2) area of operation of the terrorist groups; and (3) their capabilities and motivations. For instance, the threat to the nuclear infrastructure in the northern part of India may emanate from the terrorist and extremist groups active in Jammu & Kashmir (J&K), Al Qaeda operatives, insurgents in the northeastern states, terrorists active in the Indo-Bangladesh border region, etc. The nuclear infrastructure in the eastern part of India is vulnerable to the activities of the Naxalites, and natural disasters like a cyclone, tsunami and earthquake. The facilities in the southern part may be vulnerable to the activities of the LTTE, a cyclone, tsunami and earthquake, while the facilities of southwestern India are prone to natural disasters, religious-chauvinistic elements and attack from the sea. The facilities in the northwestern part are vulnerable to attack from across the border. While Pakistani missiles can target most of the facilities located in the northern and central part of India, Chinese missiles can theoretically reach every part of India. A realistic assessment of the intent of these sources of threat would provide a clear picture on the gravity of the threat.

Al Qaeda and Other Terrorist Groups Active in J&K

Al Qaeda is the only terrorist organisation which is believed to have the capacity to resort to nuclear terrorism, if it desires to do so. The 9/11 incident is a demonstration of its intent and reach. However, while no direct act of terrorism in India by Al Qaeda has been reported yet, its members and many pro-Al Qaeda, Pakistani pan-Islamic *jihadi* organisations have been active in Indian territory, especially in J&K, since 1993. These are the Harkat-ul-Mujahideen (HuM), the Harkat-ul-Jihad-al-Islami (HUJI), the Lashkar-e-Tayyeba (LeT), and

Jaish-e-Mohammad (JeM). The HUJI of Bangladesh, known as HUJI (B), has been active in Indian territory since 9/11. These groups believe in Osama bin Laden's religious call to consider it a duty to acquire WMD but other indigenous Kashmir separatist groups like the Jammu and Kashmir Liberation Front (JKLF) and All-Party Hurriyat Conference (APHC) have not shown interest in WMD.[38]

Before 9/11, Al Qaeda's attitude towards India or even Kashmir hardly figured in its statements. Since 9/11, and with the evolution of the Indo-US strategic partnership, references of threats to India have been more frequent. The US support to India on Kashmir, and India's relations with Israel are other major reasons for this. In an audio message disseminated in April 2006 in the wake of the visit of President George Bush to Afghanistan, India and Pakistan in March 2006, Bin Laden projected global *jihad* as directed against the "anti-Islam conspiracy of the Crusaders (Christians), the Jewish people and the Hindus."[39] Previously, there had never been a reference to Hinduism in his pronouncements. But, equally surprisingly, the reference to Hindus has not figured in subsequent statements. Though the exact interest of Al Qaeda in nuclear terrorism is not known, documents found in Afghanistan reveal that while Al Qaeda's efforts to make nuclear weapons are less than adequate, it is determined to get them and willing to use them.[40] One report says that the idea of attacks on nuclear power stations by Al Qaeda, perceived to be raised in the early stages of the planning of the 9/11 attacks, was vetoed, apparently by Bin Laden himself, perhaps because of the enormous resources and sophisticated technology required.[41] But this does not discount the probability of Al Qaeda acquiring such a capability in the future. In any case, with the level of technological expertise it has, it can easily fabricate an RDD or IND. The same is the case of other smaller *jihadi* groups. Therefore, the northern part of India is vulnerable to the designs of Al Qaeda and its associate groups. They can easily attempt sabotage of a facility, fire rockets or throw hand grenades into the facility. At the extreme, they can attempt a suicidal attack similar to 9/11 – hijacking of an aircraft and crashing it on the premises of a nuclear facility.

But how realistic is this threat and what kind of damage would it entail ? This aspect needs special attention. In the aftermath of 9/11, many studies have been conducted on the probability and consequences of an aircraft crashing into a nuclear facility. Nuclear regulatory officials in the US admit that initial containment structures were not deliberately designed to withstand the impact of large commercial aircraft. It was not seen as a threat then. But nuclear industry officials emphasise that the material strength of containment structures would be able to withstand such an eventuality. A report commissioned by the US Nuclear Energy Institute, the Electric Power Research Institute (EPRI), in June 2002 determined that containment buildings "can safely protect the reactor against most commercial aircraft." In December 2002, EPRI reported the results of a related study in which it simulated the impact of a Boeing 767-400 into four types of structures: containment buildings, spent fuel storage pools, spent fuel dry cask storage facilities and spent fuel transportation containers. The tests showed that though the containment building experienced "some crushing and spilling of the concrete" and the spent fuel pools suffered "localized crushing and cracking of the concrete wall," all the simulations showed that the aircraft was not able to breach the protection structures.[42] Edwin Lyman, a nuclear physicist, assessed that the engines of large aircraft travelling at high speeds "would penetrate the containment, leading to a fuel spill within the building and most likely to severe jet fuel fire and explosion."[43]

In India, in the aftermath of 9/11, there was a lot of apprehension on the issue of an aircraft crashing into nuclear facilities. To assess whether Indian nuclear plants can withstand an aircraft crash, one needs to know how strong the containment buildings are. The containment buildings have concrete walls, with a minimum thickness of four feet. Reactors like the Kaiga-1 and 2, Rajasthan-3 and 4 and Tarapur-3 and 4 are housed in double-domed structures. The domes of these pressurised heavy water reactors (PHWRs) are constructed using the microsilica-based high performance concrete. They also have other added safety features like an automatic, quick acting poison injection system to shut down the reactor in an emergency, and micro-processor-based systems for reactor protection and control.[44] However, the containment structures of old commercial reactors like Tarapur are not as robust as those of modern reactors. Though Indian scientists have made extensive modifications in the safety structure of the reactor, its weak containment building might not withstand a large airplane crash. While the issue of crashing a hijacked aircraft on the facility seems a simple one, the chances of it crashing on the exact location depends upon the expertise of the hijacker. Even the degree of destruction of the facility depends upon the quantum of fuel in the aircraft. For instance, a civilian aircraft hijacked soon after the take-off stage would cause more damage to the facility as it would be carrying a large amount of fuel. Thus, the probability and consequences of an aircraft crashing into a Indian nuclear facility depend upon factors like the design of the containment building, the distance of the facility from the air base, the kind of aircraft used, and the technical expertise of the terrorists. Of course, any such incident would cause huge damage to life and property; it would result in large scale nuclear contamination or an explosion. The probability of such an occurrence can be reduced by the deployment of advanced systems around sensitive nuclear facilities.

Reports in the media have claimed that the Atomic Energy Commission was seeking "no-fly zones" over nuclear installations to prevent terrorist attacks from the air[45]. Within a month after 9/11, New Delhi promulgated no-fly zone restrictions around nuclear power plants but these have not been strictly implemented yet. Surprisingly, even today, aircraft fly over BARC. Also, it is uncertain whether these facilities are adequately protected by anti-aircraft defences. Nevertheless, security at India's nuclear installations has been improved in many other ways. The Indian Coast Guard deploys additional boats off the coast of Bombay to guard BARC. Also requisition for additional anti-aircraft guns was made for deployment to the Narora Atomic Power plant in Rajasthan and for two atomic power plants in southern India.[46]

Naxalites

The second grave threat to Indian nuclear facilities would be from the Naxalites. The Naxalites are active in states like Chhattisgarh, Uttar Pradesh, Bihar, Karnataka, Kerala, Uttaranchal, Tamil Nadu, and Andhra Pradesh where many of India's nuclear facilities are located. By 1980, it was estimated that around 30 Naxalite groups were active, with a combined membership of 30, 000. A 2004 Home Ministry estimate puts the numbers at that time as 9,300 hardcore underground cadres, holding around 6,500 regular weapons, besides a large number of unlicensed country-made arms.[47] More recent figures put the strength of the movement at 15,000, and claim that the guerrillas control an estimated one-fifth of India's forests, as well as being active in 160 of the country's 604 administrative districts.[48] Though they haven't yet undertaken a large scale terrorist strike, their tactics, motivation and capabilities suggest that they could sabotage a facility in their area of activity. They can cause harm to uranium mines located in their area of operation by simply destroying the infrastructure, and capturing and diverting the raw materials to smugglers. They are known for targeting government offices, police stations, railroad tracks, jails and government officials but no such attempt has been made on nuclear facilities. Map 3 shows the distribution of nuclear facilities and the Naxal affected states in India.

Map 3
Naxal Affected States and Distribution of Nuclear Facilities in India

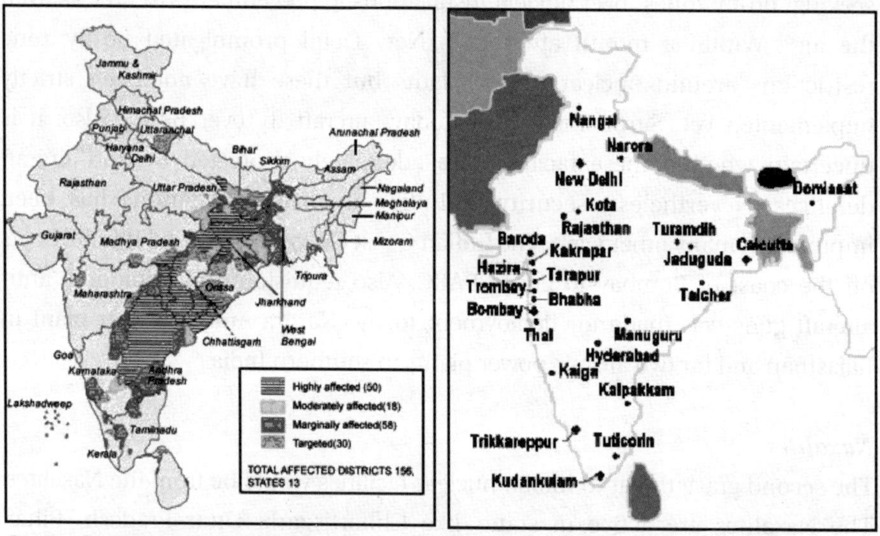

Source: http://pacificempire.org.nz/wp-content/uploads/2006/12/naxalite-affected-areas-in-india.jpg, and http://images.google.co.in

The Jaduguda uranium mine located in Jharkhand state is frequently in the news for alleged radiological material smuggling and is known to be the hotbed of the Naxalites. The Kaiga nuclear power plant in Karnataka was in the news when Union Home Minister Shivaraj Patil reportedly stated in July 2007 that there was a grave threat from the Naxalites and terrorists to the facility. The police conducted repeated combing operations in the forest region near Kaiga and in nearby Joida *taluk* to check possible intrusions of the Naxalites.[49] The recent media reports suggest that the Naxals are quietly expanding their base in states like J&K, Gujarat, Rajasthan, Himachal Pradesh and Meghalaya.[50]

However, it is difficult to assess the level of awareness of the Naxalites about nuclear technology and radiation effects. Also, it is not known how far the Naxalites are involved in radiological material smuggling. Irrespective of all the speculation about their intentions, the Naxalites must be aware of the repercussions of attacking a nuclear facility and the consequent release of radiation which, in turn, would hinder their activity in the area. Therefore, they may not take the extreme step of attacking a reactor that would release radiation; they might attack the security personnel or steal some equipment, more for impact and show of strength, than to cause actual damage. Also, if they commit any such extreme incident, governmental repression and counter-measures would be severe, thereby threatening their very survival.

Threats from Beyond the Border

The third category of threat that the Indian nuclear facilities might face is the possibility of an attack from across the border. Most of the neighbouring countries are politically unstable and extremist groups have a strong hold in these countries. Theoretically, during the time of domestic turmoil, terrorist groups may get hold of nuclear or radiological devices and use them against India. Also, the nexus between the state and extremist groups in different countries of the region is well known; therefore, chances of state-sponsored nuclear terrorism cannot be ruled out.

The first country in this context that attracts attention is Pakistan. The political situation in Pakistan is in a state of flux. Though the leadership proclaims that its nuclear arsenals are safe and well protected, owing to the chaotic political conditions, their safety and security is bound to raise apprehensions. Since 9/11, the number of terrorist incidents like suicide bombing, assassination, and political strife has increased phenomenally in Pakistan. The influence of extremist forces on the Pakistan Army is an undisputed fact. Since the assassination of Benazir Bhutto, violence has flared up across the country. It is expected that the tussle between the democratic forces and the current regime in Pakistan would continue and may lead to further deterioration of the situation. To distract popular attention from the domestic issues, and for its survival, the regime or any leader might resort to the extreme step of bringing the nuclear issue to the forefront.Mark Thompson, while branding Pakistan as the "least stable nuclear state," warns that "if Pakistan slides into total chaos and its military seems on the verge of losing control of its nuclear stockpiles, US troops will dash in to secure them. The trouble is, US officials say they don't know all the secret locations ... ."[51]

The other neighbouring country that can be a cause of concern for India in terms of nuclear terrorism is Bangladesh which is developing a "peaceful" and "transparent" nuclear energy programme.[52] Though Bangladesh is relatively less unstable than Pakistan, many extremist groups have a hold there and pose a serious threat to India. There are many instances of smuggling of radiological materials across the Indo-Bangladesh border by the terrorist groups harbouring in Bangladesh.

Among the non-state entities from outside the border, Al Qaeda and the LTTE can pose potential threats to the Indian nuclear infrastructure. While Al Qaeda's attack would focus on the northern nuclear facilities, the southern facilities are vulnerable to targeting by the LTTE which has recently started its own air wing. Another cause of concern is the status and security of the Pakistani nuclear weapons. They "could be vulnerable to theft, illicit transfer, or unintentional use if the army's discipline and command and control structure faltered"[53] and could be directed against India. Even their inadvertent or accidental use inside Pakistan would also affect India, as the radiation will spread across the border.

Threats From Fundamentalist Groups

The fourth is the threat from the religious fundamentalist and apocalyptic groups. But in India, most of these groups are deeply nationalistic and consider nuclear weapons or facilities as national wealth, and a matter of national pride. Therefore, they would not cause any harm to the nation's nuclear infrastructure. In fact, it is these nationalistic forces who for long had been demanding that New Delhi acquire nuclear weapons. Even sectarian violence may not be directed against nuclear facilities as was seen during the Godhra incident in Gujarat. Gujarat has a history of sectarian (communal) violence, going back to decades even before Indian independence in 1947, but there is no evidence of a single incident ever being aimed at the nuclear infrastructure in the state. During the visit of US President Bush to India in March 2006, Muslims staged anti-US demonstrations in Lucknow, Mumbai and Hyderabad. There were reports that sections of the Muslims – particularly in Mumbai – shouted pro-Bin Laden slogans.[54] But beyond that, they do not have the means or motivation to cause any grave harm to the nuclear infrastructure. Student activist organisations that are opposing nuclear weapons and India's relations with the US might, at best, go to the extent of staging demonstrations, but not beyond that.

Natural Disasters

The fifth is the threat from nature. Most nuclear plants are located in coastal regions. These facilities, therefore, may be affected by cyclones, tsunamis, earthquakes, etc. Though nothing serious happened to the reactor, the recent earthquake in Japan had definitely shaken everyone's imagination.[55] Any such massive natural disaster may cause severe damage to Indian facilities, and result in release of radiation. Also, the post-disaster period is critical as the saboteurs may take advantage of the situation. A coastal location is convenient for the construction of a nuclear plant but the location of these facilities has complicated their security planning against external threats.[56] Therefore, the in-built safety structures of the facilities is of prime importance. If the security arrangements are properly in place, a facility can withstand minor threats.

Examining the Security and Safety Standards of Indian Facilities

On March, 31 2005, India ratified the Convention on Nuclear Safety and submitted its first National Report (September 2007) for review by the contracting parties, pursuant to Article 5 of the Convention that entered into force on October, 24 1996. The report demonstrates how the Government of India has fulfilled its obligations under Articles 6 through 19 of the Convention. The report says that all operating nuclear installations in India are subject to "continuous regulatory appraisal of safety as per the established requirements" and "utmost attention is given to safety in every stage of realisation of nuclear power plants to ensure safety of operating personnel, the public as well as the environment." The "principle of safety is the overriding priority," and the measures are "comprehensive," covering the entire gamut of activities i.e. siting, design, construction, commissioning, operation and decommissioning, etc. according to the report.

However, Charles D. Ferguson, a fellow for science and technology of the US Council on Foreign Relations, has conducted a comprehensive study on the military and terrorist threats against Indian civilian nuclear facilities, wherein he argues that the sheer complexity of the Indian "three-pronged plan could complicate management of ensuring adequate security throughout the programme."[57] He reiterates that the differential reactor design "would require detailed attention to differences in vulnerability to various modes of attack." The main findings of his study are as follows:

1. CANDU-type reactors, such as the Indian PHWRs, have certain safety features that make them capable of surviving an attack or sabotage. Containment buildings having a minimum of four-foot thick concrete walls typically enclose CANDU reactors.
2. India's most recently built PHWRs have an added safety feature: double-domed containment structures. These PHWRs are the Kaiga-I and 2 reactors, the Rajasthan-3 and 4 reactors, and the Tarapur-3 and 4 reactors.
3. The containment structures of the Tarapur reactors are not as robust as those of more modern boiling water reactors (BWRs). A weak containment building might not withstand the crash of a large airplane.
4. The Russian supplied VVER-1000 reactors at Kudankulam have relatively large coolant-to-power ratio and some inherent protection in the event of a loss of coolant incident. But the VVER-1000 has some inherent weaknesses. Vulnerabilities include: steam lines and isolation valves too close together, which a single blast could knock out; the control room is

located at the lower level of the reactor building, potentially prompting quick evacuation if the containment is breached, thus, minimising the amount of time operators have to control the reactor; and relatively weak containment structures that an airplane might penetrate.

5. Many research reactors in India do not use containment buildings, and if they do, the containments tend to be not as strong as those surrounding commercial reactors. Research reactors, especially those at universities, also tend to have less security forces than commercial power plants. Also, most of the Indian research reactors are usually located within institutions, and before the Indo-US civil nuclear cooperation, they were performing both civilian and military tasks. Security at these dual-use institutions seems strong because of their role in India's military programme. However, because of their dual-use role, military or terrorist attackers might find it attractive to strike such facilities.
6. The decommissioned reactors, while not operating, could still present potential targets because of the possible presence of radioactive materials on-site. At BARC, at Trombay, there are two operating research reactors, and three decommissioned reactors (Purnima-1, critical assembly, Purnima-2 LWR, and Zerlina PHWR).
7. An expanding stockpile of weapon-usable plutonium can increase the risk of terrorists building an improvised nuclear explosive. Currently, India uses the CIRUS and Dhruva research reactors to produce plutonium. Also, BARC contains a plutonium separation plant that can process 30 to 50 tonnes of spent fuel annually, and a plutonium weapons component facility.
8. The pool at Tarapur-1 was initially designed to store at most 72 metric tonnes of spent fuel. But it now contains more than twice that amount. Storing more than the originally designed amount of spent fuel can increase the risk of the spent fuel catching fire in the event of a loss of coolant incident. Also the majority of India spent fuel pools at PHWRs most likely follow the CANDU design. The typical CANDU plant has its spent fuel pool outside the containment building, thus, it is more exposed to attack than a BWR pool.

9. Presently, India uses the PUREX reprocessing method, which is considered to be proliferation-prone because it completely separates plutonium from the self-protecting highly radioactive materials in spent fuel. Thieves or terrorists can carry separated plutonium without suffering near-term harm to health.
10. As India reprocesses plutonium in bulk at Tarapur and Kalpakkam, there is likely to be loss of material unaccounted for (MUF). MUF can add up to many kilograms of plutonium not properly tracked, especially in a bulk handling facility. As India's rate of reprocessing and production of plutonium-based fuel increases, the likelihood of large amounts of MUF will increase.
11. The high level radioactive waste storage areas also poses another danger to an attack. India has developed the capability to immobilise the liquid waste in glass. Such immobilisation would create hard to disperse radioactive materials and would provide significant protection against radioactivity release from an attack on a high-level waste storage facility. To make effective use of this protection, India would have to operate the immobilisation at a rate commensurate with the production of liquid waste.

India's National Report to the Convention on Nuclear Safety, September 2007, mentions that systematic approaches are followed in the design, commissioning, operation, performance, quality, and safety of the Indian NPPs.[58] They are as follows:

Site Selection and Construction: Before the setting up of a nuclear plant, detailed investigations are made for assessing the seismic history and geological characteristics of the region, possibility of natural threats like floods, high tides, wind effects, etc. Safety during the construction is also maintained through stringent quality assurance during material selection, testing, component fabrication, civil construction, site election, assembly and commissioning.

Design of Plants: Well-defined principles are followed in the design of the nuclear power plants to provide the required safety features, adopting the principles of defence-in-depth, diversity and redundancy. India's NPPs are constructed in accordance with the "design intent, and with required quality of workmanship" to ensure the highest quality. This implies a safety philosophy wherein several lines of defences are created so that radioactive fission products generated in the reactor are effectively contained under all circumstances.

Commissioning: Commissioning of the systems is made to test and demonstrate the adequacy of each system and the plant as a whole by actual performance tests to meet the design intent carried out before commencing the operation of the plant.

Regulatory Framework and Operation: Operation of the plant is carried out as per approved procedures by defining the operational limits and conditions for various system parameters. The technical specifications for operation are thoroughly reviewed and approved by the Atomic Energy Regulatary Board (AERB). Further, the AERB, through formal clearances, authorises actions stipulating specific conditions at various stages of the plant. These include site approval, review and approval of safety design of systems and authorisations for construction, commissioning, operation and safety review during the operational phase. The regulatory framework of nuclear facilities in India seems robust. The design of systems, structures and components and the plant layout is carried out with applicable codes and guides as stipulated by the regulatory body and as per the prevalent international practices aimed at limiting human errors during normal operating conditions and maintenance.

Performance Monitoring: Performance monitoring of maintenance activities with respect to the human factors are carried out on a regular basis. The man-machine interface is designed to provide the operators with comprehensive and easily manageable information. Interlocks and automatic actions are so designed that only those actions are required to be taken by the operator where adequate time is available for taking necessary action. The control panels are ergonomically designed and the working areas and environment of the site are designed with due consideration of providing personnel comfort.

Waste Management: As per the report, all nuclear power plant sites in India are self-sufficient in the management of the radioactive waste generated. Adequate facilities have been provided for handling, treatment and disposal of wastes generated from plant operation at these sites. Management of radioactive wastes is carried out in conformity with the regulatory guidelines based on internationally accepted principles.

Quality Assurance Programme of the nuclear industry in India has evolved following national and international standards and codes of practices. The Engineering Directorate is responsible for the design, development and engineering activities. Design from concept to completion, is undertaken, reviewed, evaluated, analysed and validated thoroughly. Design and development processes and activities are performed following the Quality Management System Manual of the Engineering Directorate of the Utility, developed in line with the "Corporate Management System Document."

Periodic Safety Review: A comprehensive periodic safety review of operational and safety performance of NPPs which includes factors like changes in safety standards, ageing, new information, etc. is carried out at the time of renewal of authorisation or major refurbishment or for plant life extension. Such reviews bring out the requirements for major modification and safety upgradation, particularly in older plants, which were built to earlier safety standards. As per the report, all the older NPPs have undergone such safety upgrades.

Public Awareness: Regular training courses are arranged by each NPP for the general public in that area, sometimes by inviting them in batches to the plant. The course contents include an introduction to atomic energy, safety in the nuclear industry and the emergency organisation in that nuclear power plant. As a part of this public awareness programme, visits to the Emergency Control Centres and the Environmental Survey Laboratories are also arranged. As a means of creating better public awareness, a short list of "DOs" and "DON'Ts" during a nuclear emergency is being distributed to the public.

There is no duality of opinion regarding the commitment of Indian scientists to ensure the safety of the plants over the decades. The nuclear sector is the only one where each employee is subjected to constant and periodic monitoring. The plants follow the "zoning system" with regular contamination checks of personnel and equipment. To minimise airborne radioactivity, special ventilation systems are designed and installed. Radiation levels in various plant areas are continuously monitored. However, there should be "no room for complacency" as India has to go a long way in its march on the nuclear path. When it is planning for more power plants, implying increased nuclear fuel cycle activities, "the safety concerns must be viewed with greater seriousness and urgency."[59] Though their authenticity may be debatable there have been many media reports regarding the emission of radiation from the Kakrapara Atomic Power Station which is allegedly three times more than the international norm.[60] While the government releases no information about these accidents, Dhirendra Sharma, a scientist who has written extensively on India's atomic-power projects, has compiled figures based on his own reporting. "An estimated 300 incidents of a serious nature have occurred, causing radiation leaks and physical damage to workers," he says.[61] During the 1990s, the then AERB Chairman A. Gopalakrishnan led the charge that safety of Indian nuclear facilities had fallen short.[62] He said that "there were 130 safety-related issues in various nuclear facilities, of which 95 belong to the NPC alone."

In the aftermath of the Chernobyl disaster, Prime Minister Rajiv Gandhi asked for a complete review of the safety standard and emergency preparedness plan of Indian nuclear plants and then only did he agree to sanction new nuclear power projects. The Department of Atomic Energy (DAE) consulted the chief secretaries of the states where nuclear installations were located, along with the district administrations concerned, and drew up comprehensive plans to deal with any such emergency. Detailed plans are prepared for each site in conjunction with the district collector and his principal officers and these are updated periodically. Since then, plant emergency exercises are carried out four times a year, site emergency exercises are carried out once a year, and off-site emergency exercises once in two years. Whatever the standard of safety measures in place in Indian nuclear facilities, one thing is clear – there is lot of concern for, and constant attempt by the concerned authorities to upgrade, the arrangements.

The Legal Mechanism in Place

Though India does not have a single and overarching integrated legislative provision to address the issue of nuclear terrorism in the country, several national Acts on export controls and import restrictions, trade regulation, atomic energy policy, industrial policy resolutions, licensing policies and international obligations emanating from its adherence to the international conventions, provide an exhaustive legal framework to address this issue. Starting from the formulation of the Explosive Substances Act in 1908[63] and the Atomic Energy Act in 1962[64] to the promulgation of the Weapons of Mass Destruction and their Delivery System (Prohibition of Unlawful Activities) Act in 2005[65] and the Disaster Management Act 2005[66], India has consistently endeavoured to restrict possible pilferage of explosive and radioactive materials. However, all these provisions, including the Special Chemical, Organisms, Materials, Equipment and Technology (SCOMET) list of the Export-Import Act, Customs Act of 1962, Chemical Weapons Convention Act of 2000, Biological Weapons Toxin Convention, Environment Protection Act, POTA, etc. were actually designed for specific aspects and controls. Moreover, except the WMD Act 2005, none of these laws is actually concerned with non-proliferation and terrorism directly.

India's effort in the field of export control of radiological materials has a long history.[67] The country has been involved in the commercial exploitation of atomic minerals since the 1930s. The British had interest in radioactive minerals in the southern part of the country and even encouraged the state of Travancore to remain separate from the Indian state. Meanwhile, a Research Committee on Atomic Energy had been set up in 1946, even before India became independent. It recommended that the Government of India regulate the exploitation and export of atomic minerals. Since the promulgation of the Atomic Energy Act 1948, the exploitation, research, import and export of atomic minerals and technology has been under the strict control of the national government. The Atomic Energy Acts of 1962 and 1995 specially govern the ownership, use and trade of atomic minerals and technologies. Other institutional bases for export controls on WMD are the Indian Export-Import Policy, Industrial Policy Resolutions, Foreign Trade

(Development and Regulation) Act 1992, etc. The Department of Atomic Energy (DAE) is the nodal agency for review and evaluation of policy details.

In 2005, India promulgated the landmark Weapons of Mass Destruction (Prohibition of Unlawful Activities) Act[68] which crystallised the nation's responsibility to control illegal export of materials and technology related to creation and delivery of WMD. The Act declares that "India is determined to safeguard its national security as a Nuclear Weapons State" and is "committed to the objective of global nuclear disarmament." The jurisdiction of the Act extends to the whole of India and applies to the entire citizenry and the foreigners in India, companies and corporate bodies, all means of transport and government servants. The provisions of the Act apply to export, import, transfer, retransfer, transit and trans-shipment of material and technology. A person shall be punishable with imprisonment for a term of not less than five years which may extend to life imprisonment, if he attempts to contravene the provisions of Sections 8 and 10 of the Act which deal with prohibitions regarding WMD. The Act contains 'catch-all' provisions and is definitely an addition to the numerous domestic regulations already in force to criminalise proliferation of WMD. However, India has a long history of formulating good laws but bad enforcement. Also, many weaknesses are inherent in the Act and can cleverly be manipulated. For example, the definition of non-state actor – "a person or entity not acting under the lawful authority of any country" – borrowed from the United Nations Security Council (UNSC) Resolution 1540 is inadequate as many lawfully registered agencies carry out unlawful activities. The need of the hour is to stay abreast of emerging challenges.

The Government of India has also enacted the "Disaster Management Act, 2005" which provides guidelines for the effective management of disasters, including accidents involving nuclear power plants. As per the provisions, the National Disaster Management Authority (NDMA) has been established at the national level, with the prime minister as its chairman. The NDMA has the responsibility for laying down policies, plans and guidelines for disaster management for ensuring timely and effective response to any disaster. In line with the above, the National Plan, State Plans and District Plans are drawn up by the respective authorities constituted for the purpose. In accordance with the Crisis Management Plan evolved by the government, the DAE has been identified as the nodal authority in respect of nuclear/radiological emergencies in the public domain. For this purpose, a Crisis Management Group (CMG) has been set up. The group is chaired by the additional secretary, DAE, and has members from various arms of the DAE and AERB. The DAE maintains a database to track exporters and importers of nuclear materials.

At the multilateral and bilateral levels, New Delhi is involved in many preventive and cooperative arrangements at both regional and international fora. At the regional level, India is a signatory to the South Asian Association for Regional Cooperation (SAARC) Regional Convention on Suppression of Terrorism[69] and the Additional Protocol[70] (January 6, 2004) to the convention, which prohibits and binds each contracting party to "refrain from organising, instigating, assisting or participating in acts of civil strife or terrorist acts in another state" while criminalising any activity relating to the collection or acquisition of funds for the purpose of committing terrorist acts by taking measures to prevent and suppress financing of such acts. However, the convention doesn't refer to nuclear related terrorism.

At the international level, India is party to many multilateral arrangements to arrest nuclear terrorism. India has ratified the Convention on the Physical Protection of Nuclear Material, signed at Vienna on March 3, 1980,[71] The convention provides a legal basis to physical protection measures for nuclear material that have been evolved over time by the International Atomic Energy Agency (IAEA). It provides a framework for international cooperation in protection against theft or unauthorised diversion of nuclear materials and obliges state parties to ensure physical protection of nuclear material during international transport. The convention reinforces India's commitment to international legal instruments against terrorism in general and nuclear terrorism in particular. India has already put in place the measures necessary to implement the provisions of the convention. India, in addition to adhering to the UNSC Resolution 1540 on the non-proliferation of weapons of mass destruction, sponsored a draft resolution on "Measures to Prevent Terrorists from Acquiring Weapons of Mass Destruction" along with other countries, which remains as a preambular reference to the resolution. The second important multilateral initiative was the adoption of an international convention addressing the threat of nuclear terrorism by the UN General Assembly on April 13, 2005, to which India is also a signatory.[72]

Also, bilaterally, India is party to many arrangements meant for restricting proliferation of WMD. India is considering the US initiated Proliferation Security Initiative (PSI) programme and is already a party in the Container Security Initiative (CSI). The proposed Indo-US civilian nuclear agreement seems to promise better cooperation in combating nuclear terrorism and strengthening nuclear safety.[73] India is party to as many as 12 international conventions and protocols on combating terrorism and attaches high priority to the formulation of international legal instruments to combat terrorism and has incorporated them in domestic legislations. As is seen, it has also played a major part in strengthening international consensus against terrorism in the UN, Non-Aligned Movement (NAM), and SAARC fora. However, India remains outside the framework of the existing multilateral non-proliferation export control regimes like the Zangger Committee, Nuclear Suppliers' Group (NSG), Australia Group (AG), Missile Technology Control Regime (MTCR) and Wassenaar Arrangement (WA).

Is India Prepared?

As per the Indian official position, the country is prepared for a response to nuclear or radiological terrorism; however, what is urgently required is a robust improvement of the existing preparedness to respond effectively to large scale nuclear and radiological emergencies. Now the question that needs to be addressed is: are the mechanisms in place competent to tackle a nuclear terror incident 'any where, any time'?

The radiation protection framework in India broadly comprises:

(1) Legal provisions.

(2)Surveillance and safety mechanisms.

(3 Emergency response mechanisms.

(4) External collaboration.

With the dawn of the nuclear era in India, the country has promulgated

Fig. 2

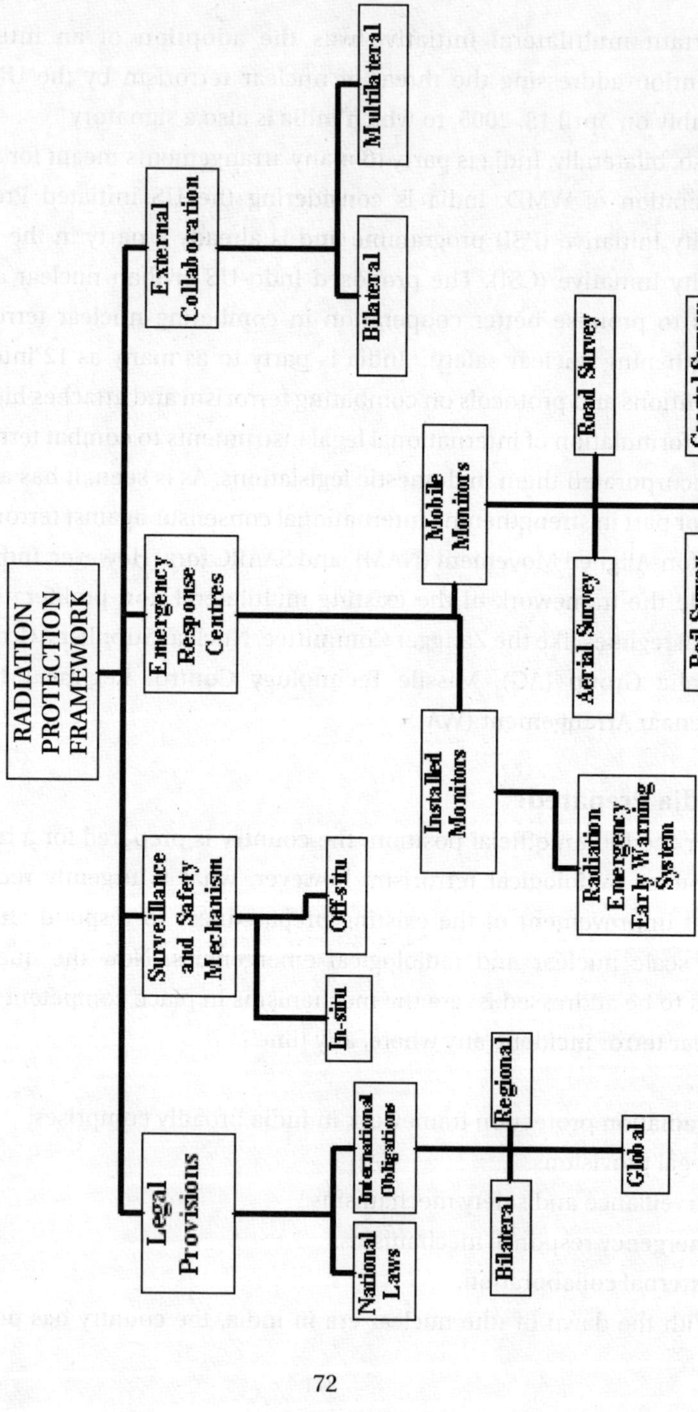
RADIATION PROTECTION FRAMEWORK
External Collaboration
Bilateral
Multilateral
Emergency Response Centres
Mobile Monitors
Installed Monitors
Aerial Survey
Road Survey
Rail Survey
Coastal Survey
Radiation Emergency Early Warning System
Surveillance and Safety Mechanism
In-situ
Off-situ
Legal Provisions
National Laws
International Obligations
Bilateral
Regional
Global

many provisions with the objective to streamline nuclear technology growth in the country in a regulated manner. Therefore, a comprehensive legal framework is already in place to restrict the misuse of the technology and resources, as has been discussed in the preceding section. Also, a plethora of safety mechanisms is in place in the nuclear facilities (already discussed in the preceding section) to contain or minimise radiation if any unwarranted situation arises. But we cannot afford to wait for a nuclear disaster to take place. A strict surveillance system is a must to track and monitor the movement of radiological materials and anti-national elements who are suspected to resort to nuclear terrorism. However, the safety mechanism at Indian nuclear facilities, as the DAE proclaims, "is on very sound footing and is constantly being strengthened."[74] Other initiatives of DAE[75] in this regard are:

1. BARC and the laboratories accredited by it, conduct countrywide personnel monitoring in about 3,000 industrial, medical, research and DAE organisations which benefit over 30,000 radiation workers annually.
2. Environmental radiation monitoring and environmental surveillance are regular features of the environmental protection programme of DAE. At different sites, the Environment Survey Labs of BARC continuously monitor the environment, and collect site related meteorological data. Sophisticated weather monitoring SODAR systems are operational at Kaiga, Kalpakkam, Tarapur and Trombay.
3. The environment around nuclear sites is well conserved. Many of the nuclear power stations have obtained Environmental Management System Certification under ISO 14001, and have won the "AERB Green Site Award". To educate the public living around nuclear power plants, public awareness programmes by DAE are organised on a regular basis.
4. The World Association of Nuclear Operators (WANO) conducts peer reviews of all the atomic power stations and the NPCIL (Nuclear Power Corporation India Ltd.) is a member of the association.
5. The AERB receives advice from another Advisory Committee, viz. Advisory Committee on Nuclear Safety (ACNS). ACNS provides recommendations on the safety codes, guides and manuals prepared for siting, design, construction, operation, quality assurance and decommissioning/life

extension of nuclear power plants which have been prepared by the respective advisory committees for each of these areas.

6. The BARC Safety Council maintains its regulatory function to ensure the safety of all plants and facilities under its purview. A comprehensive programme on radiation protection services covering all installations in power, medicine, agriculture, industry, environment, and human resources development is being carried out by the Department of Atomic Energy with full government budgetary support and commitment.
7. The Indian Association for Radiation Protection was established in the year 1968 to promote safety in the manifold uses of ionising radiation in India. It has so far conducted a number of public awareness programmes and arranged many workshops, and national and international conferences for fruitful exchange of radiation protection ideas and philosophy.

The emergency response mechanism[76] in India also seems comprehensive. A network of 18 Emergency Response Centres (ERC)[77] with skilled Emergency Response Teams (ERT) comprising the Aerial Survey Team (AST), Field Monitoring Team (FMT), Source Recovery Team (SRT), Assessment and Advisory Team (AAT), Medical Team (MT) and Bioassay Team (BT) has been established in different parts of the country, including BARC (Mumbai) as the nodal agency. In case of any such incident, an urgent response would be extended after conducting a Quick Impact Assessment (QIA) through Impact Assessment Software (IAS) specially developed in BARC to predict the impact. As per the arrangement, the ERC nearest to the site of such incident will be activated by the centralised Emergency Communication Room (ECR - Mumbai) of the Crisis Management Group (CMG) of the DAE, on receipt of confirmation. The CMG coordinates between various state and central agencies to facilitate an effective response to such emergencies. During the past few years, the first-responders – custom officials, police, fire brigade personnel and paramilitary forces – are being trained to handle radiological emergencies. State-of-the-art monitoring systems and methodology are developed and kept in readiness in various parts of the country.[78] Systems that have been already developed by India are:

1. Aerial Gamma Spectrometry System (AGSS) which can be installed in an

aircraft for quick impact assessment by aerial surveys; Aerial Monitoring Methodology is developed for the quick assessment of large scale ground contamination search for locating and identifying radioactive orphan sources, tracking of radioactive plume.

2. Environmental Radiation Monitoring with Navigational Aid (ERMNA) System for periodic mobile radiation monitoring of major cities and Emergency Planning Zones (EPZ) of nuclear power plants to generate baseline dose rate data.
3. Compact Aerial Radiation Monitoring System (CARMS) for remote aerial monitoring.
4. Environmental Radiation Monitoring Systems (Indian Environmental Radiation Monitoring Network-IERMON) with data transfer facilities to Emergency Response Centres.

To carry out effective counter-measures and rescue operations during any emergency, the Geographical Information System (GIS) developed by Indian scientists can be used to obtain the details of the shelter locations, road network, buildings, population density, water bodies, agriculture, etc. of an affected area, to initiate urgent protection actions. Mapping of the contaminated area based on an aerial survey using advanced software and satellite imagery, would be very effective for the quick implementation of counter-measures. Environmental radiation monitoring is conducted by state-of-the-art systems like CARMS, ERMNA, AGSS, etc. by aerial survey, sea road and rail routes. Till March 2007, at least 13 major aerial surveys had been conducted on different cities of the India.[79] Other counter-measures devised to reduce probable consequences are: iodine prophylaxis, sheltering, decontamination, access control, evacuation, restriction of the consumption of potentially contaminated foodstuffs, agricultural counter-measures, permanent relocation, etc.

Indian scientists have designed a few "prototype nuclear shelters" that are self-contained units with sleeping bunks for around 30 people, equipped with captive power and water supply systems[80] Toilets and decontamination modules, including waste disposal and fire-fighting systems are also part of the underground shelters. These prototype radiation-proof shelters are meant for the short-term survival of a few specially trained n-force personnel in a near-miss situation. Also keeping a nuclear eventuality in mind, the Indian government has planned to construct underground shelters, equipped with electronic networks, at different locations in the country.[81] Equipped with nuclear warheads on long-range surface-to-surface ballistic missiles, they will be directly linked to a central command of the Nuclear Defence War Council (NDWC). Using the secret electronic codes, these are intended to instantly unleash retaliatory nuclear strikes. However, the cost of a nuclear shelter is very high and it cannot be produced on a mass scale.

India is also proactive in the Regional Cooperative Agreement (RCA) for promotion of cooperative research, development and training related to nuclear science and technology among member countries of Asia and the Pacific region. India's contribution to the radiation protection activities of the RCA during the first phase (1989-92), second phase (1993-97) and third phase (1998-2002) has been praiseworthy and is expected to be much more significant in the decades to come.[82] To its credit, India has organised several workshops and training courses with the active support of the forum. But it is not known whether the RCA has any plan or initiative to devise an effective method to mitigate any unwarranted situation caused by non-state actors.

No doubt, the national effort to minimise the chances of nuclear terrorism is growing in size and scope but surprisingly a serious domestic debate on nuclear terrorism is absent. Perhaps the scientific community and the political leadership are confronted by the dilemma of public sensitivity to the nuclear issues and are deliberately trying to avoid unnecessary alarm. But the leadership – scientific, political and defence – is aware and constantly monitoring the issue. However, much more serious effort needs to be initiated to avert a nuclear disaster and to tackle a post-disaster situation. Vice Admiral V.K. Singh, director general of the Armed Forces Medical Services, said in the conference on "Medical Preparedness and Mass Casualty Management" in August 2006 in New Delhi, "We do not have the preparedness to tackle calamities such as nuclear disasters and more people could die due to confusion and lack of awareness."[83] Singh said the Indian Army had launched a process for providing such facilities at 200 of its hospitals. In the same line, National Disaster Management Authority Vice Chairman Gen. N.C. Vij, while inaugurating the conference, said that India needs to fully be prepared to tackle nuclear disasters and terror attacks. He said the country urgently needs to improve facilities such as ambulances and hospitals which can absorb a large number of patients, and trained personnel who can handle them. More urgency-management staff is required for this.

The legal-technical mechanisms that are available may not serve the purpose unless they are accompanied by an efficient implementation process. Both the citizenry and the security personnel need to be imparted basic nuclear knowledge so that any unwarranted situation can be handled. Any such event, if takes place, would cost the nation dearly. Besides loss of human life, India's national growth in the long-term would be severely hampered. India's plan and efforts for energy security through nuclear energy would also be severely thwarted as any terror incident would turn off the governmental and public perception and support. It has already been seen how the Three Mile Island accident of March 1979 restricted the US capability to expand the nuclear energy infrastructure in the country.

What Should Be Done?

As nuclear terrorism is not a single issue phenomenon, only a stringent-security or heightened-safety approach to counter it won't suffice. Nuclear discourse involves politics, security, safety, psychology, technology, and much more. A concerted approach, involving all the above aspects, would help in dealing with the menace.

From the legal point of view, India needs the legislation of a national Nuclear Technology Management Act containing clear guidelines for nuclear disaster management. The Atomic Energy Act does provide broad outlines on the management of national atomic resources, but the emerging challenges relating to terrorism need to be addressed. Though the Disaster Management Act 2005 embodies provisions for managing nuclear disasters, a dedicated policy framework with the supporting infrastructure for managing nuclear disasters would provide prompt response and expertise in meeting the challenge.

When India is planning for an ambitious expansion of its nuclear enterprise, the credibility of the security practices needs to be reassessed. Including a paramilitary guard force and a personnel reliability programme, the design basis threat (DBT — the level of threat from outside attackers and inside) saboteurs — must reflect a credible terrorism threat. The vulnerability assessment mitigation (VAM) method should be used in reevaluating the security structure of the establishment. It is expected that India must have reexamined its DBT in the light of the growing influence of terrorists in the subcontinent and put in place advanced sabotage resistance safety systems. Also, looking at the growing Naxalite activities, a Naxal-specific security arrangement for the facilities located in the Naxal-affected belt must be devised as their activities are completely different from any other form of threat.

It is interesting to know that Indian scientists have developed advanced hardware and software, some of which is already in place but the information regarding their preparedness is not publicly available. Although secrecy can protect sensitive information from the enemy, too much secrecy can also silence the questioning of relevant issues that leads to improvements in security. Openness to self-criticism is equally important. The security of the nuclear infrastructure can be better strengthened through cooperative security frameworks. India is working in cooperation with the US, IAEA and other relevant entities. A relevant precedent is the opening up of India's civilian nuclear programme to outside peer review of the safety systems and operational practices at its nuclear power plants. The World Association of Nuclear Operators (WANO) has conducted several such confidential reviews in India. A WANO-like security peer review could confidentially identify shortcomings in India's security system for its nuclear infrastructure.

The policy-makers need to be convinced that nuclear terror is an "uncertain reality"; therefore, India needs to master a credible "attribution capability". In 2000, the Defence Threat Reduction Agency (DTRA) of the US Department of Defence initiated a nuclear attribution programme for developing an "operational, rapid deployment ground sample collection capability."[84] The DTRA has also developed "a domestic ground sample collection capability, a forensics lab process, and an exercise programme to sustain the sample collection and lab forensics." The Domestic Nuclear Detection Office (DNDO) of the Department of Homeland Security plays an important role in developing US capabilities in this area. India, on the lines of US preparedness, needs to embark on an R&D programme for nuclear attribution technology. The attribution capability, backed by an efficient reference database, intelligence and law enforcement capabilities would help India to identify the likely suspects or culprits to preempt a follow-on measure. In this regard, Indian scientists are capable of collecting air, water and soil samples of the affected area for examination at short notice. The biological dosimeters with field applicability to assess the extent of biological damage in a disaster situation have also been installed in limited numbers. As a part of this programme, some radiation detection devices or sensors have already been installed at vital places like airports and sea crossings but installing these devices on a massive scale at every place across the country becomes an issue of resources availability.

Presently, public perception on anything nuclear is somewhat blurred, not necessarily because the technology is "brutish" but because of the nature of information and the way it is disseminated. This simply vindicates the criticism that there is lopsided management of information on nuclear technology. At every stage in the development of nuclear energy – fissile material mining, enrichment, energy generation, and waste management – information is necessitated and also generated. Thus, the nuclear industry has unique information preservation issues. India needs to frame a Nuclear Information Management (NIM) programme. It needs to preserve the records and knowledge of how to use the information in a sustainable way. The creation of a national nuclear archive can be also considered.

Information professionals need to consider not only how and what information is to be preserved, they must also know *how to access, and use* it, while nullifying every chance of its leakage. Also, at regular intervals, research information storage systems need to be assessed. The scientific community has a bigger role in managing nuclear information. It is they who know what is what. It is their obligation to keep science away from ideology and politics.

The political establishments (both the government and the opposition), devoid of all electoral gimmicks, must frame unbiased national nuclear policies and update the citizenry with the necessary information on the discourse. The media, intelligentsia and academia have multiple roles in the effective management of nuclear information. It is they who should investigate the available information and bring the reality to light. However, they must shed their political affiliations while interpreting the investigation on the information and its dissemination for public scrutiny. Again, with the flood of information caused by the information technology (IT) revolution, it is a stupendous task for them to pick up the correct and relevant information.

The role of civil society is equally important in the effective management of nuclear information. Every concerned citizen, non-govermental organisation (NGO), social group, and think-tank, with their intrusive enquiry, must evaluate the objectivity and authenticity of all available information before articulating their perceptions. They must demand accountability of the information provided. Therefore, a specially designed curriculum on nuclear technology and energy is needed to be framed in order to make people understand the truth. This would reduce the likelihood any kind of hoax situation being created by the terrorists. India can think about incorporating the subject of nuclear technology in the enducational curriculum, from the school to the university level. Public awareness initiatives for imparting the correct perspectives on the effects of radiation and on a nuclear disaster and its management need to be initiated urgently.

Most important is the readiness of the medical establishment and the equipment at their disposal. It is shocking to know that the medical syllabus in India does not include any such course. Neither do the police training centres provide any such training to the personnel. Like in the fire brigade stations, a first response team needs to be created and kept in readiness at various locations, especially in mega cities. An appropriate "first action manual" needs to be prepared for the necessary guidelines. Hospitals in different metropoles and big cities urgently require to be equipped for treating radiation victims and emergencies. Specialised trauma control hospitals need be developed. Radiomodulatory drugs for post-exposure treatment need urgent attention. Endogenous or exogenous radioprotectors, free radical scavenging drugs of high efficiency and nucleotide modifiers need to be developed. Since tackling a nuclear disaster is not an easy task, international collaborations need be initiated and strengthened for free exchange of information and collaborative research.

Finally, it needs to be understood that the nuclear discourse concens politics more than science, psychology more than physics; therefore, any effort to arrest the possible chances of a nuclear terror incident must be all inclusive.

Notes

1. “Nuclear Terrorism Top Fear, Survey Says,” United Press International, January 4,2008.
2. Arun Kumar, “Training Programmes in India for Safety and Security of Radioactive Sources,” Radiological Safety Division, Atomic Energy Regulatory Board, Mumbai.
3. “Security Beefed up at BARC”, *The Times of India* (New Delhi), August 13, 2006.
4. “India Upgraded Security at Nuclear Facilities Amid Terror Warnings” http://www.spacewar.com/2006/060905173711.nmt76wrz.html,05 September 2006
5. “India-US Nuclear Deal Makes Indian Nuclear Plants Really Vulnerable to Islamic Terror Targets: Indian Home Minister Shivraj Patil,” http://www.indiadaily.com/editorial/14359.asp, November 22, 2006.
6. *The Hindu*, August 16, 2006.
7. *The Hindustan Times*, August 22, 2006.
8. “Radioactive Isotopes Stolen From TISCO,” http://sify.com/news/fullstory.php?id =13227087, August 17, 2003.
9. “Uranium-Based Ash Analyser Stolen from CMPDIL Complex in Ranchi,” http://www.paktribune.com/news/index.shtml?174293, April 6, 2007.
10. “Search on for Missing Uranium-Based Ash Analyzer,” *The Hindu*, December 24, 2006.
11. “CBI to go Ahead with Uranium Theft Case Probe”, *The Indian Express*, July 30, 1998.
12. “Indian Politician Accused of Smuggling Uranium,” http://news.bbc.co.uk/1/hi/world/ south_asia/113674.stm, June 16, 1998.
13. Ibid.
14. “Uranium Smugglers Caught in India,” http://news.bbc.co.uk/1/hi/world/ south_asia/1512077.stm, August 27, 2001.
15. http://govinfo.library.unt.edu/ota/Ota_5/DATA/1977/9586.PDF
16. Lyudmila Zaitseva and Friedrich Steinhausler, “International Dimension of Illicit Trafficking in Nuclear and other Radioactive Material,” paper prepared for EU High-

Level International Scientific Conference on Physical Protection, Salzburg, Austria, September 8-13, 2002, p.3, http://www.numat.at/list%20of%20papers/zaitseva.pdf.

17. Andrew Prosser, "Nuclear Trafficking Routes: Dangerous Trends in South Asia," Centre for Defence Information, November 24, 2004, p.9, http://www.cdi.org/PDFs/TraffickingSmuggling.pdf
18. Database on Nuclear Smuggling, Theft and Orphan Radiation Sources (DSTO); Friedrich Steinhausler and Lyudmila Zaitseva, Division of Physics and Biophysics, Salzburg University, 2004; "IAEA Illicit Trafficking Database (ITDB)" available at: http://www.iaea.org/NewsCenter/Features/RadSources/PDF/fact_figures2006.pdf
19. Ibid.
20. "Nuclear Black Markets: Pakistan, A.Q. Khan and the Rise of Proliferation Networks, A Net Assessment," International Institute for Strategic Studies (London), May 2, 2007.
21. Arun Kumar, S.P. Agarwal, A.N. Nandakumar, R.Kannan and B.C. Bhatt, "Training Programmes in India for Safety and Security of Radioactive Sources," International Conference on Physical Protection, Salzburg, Austria, September 8-13, http://www.numat.at/list%20of%20papers/arunkumar.pdf
22. Kumar, et al, "Safety and Security of Radioactive Materials – the Indian Scenario," Bhaba Atomic Research Centre, 1998.
23. Kumar, et al. n. 21.
24. Rajesh M. Basrur and Friedrich Steinhausler, "Nuclear and Radiological Terrorism Threats for India: Risk Potential and Countermeasures," http://jps.lanl.gov/vol1_iss1/3-Threats_for_India.pdf
25. Interview with A. Gopalkrishnan, former chairman of the Atomic Energy Regulatory Board of the Government of India, as quoted in Kishore Kuchibhotla and Matthew McKinzie, "Nuclear Terrorism and Nuclear Accidents in South Asia," http://www.stimson.org/southasia/pdf/reducingnukes-section5.pdf, p. 30
26. Adnan Gill, "How Secure Are Indian Nukes?," http://www.pakistanlink.com/Opinion/2006/Oct06/27/09.HTM, October 31, 2007.
27. "'Armed Men' Enter Indian Nuclear Plant," http://www.bangkokpost.com/breaking_news/breakingnews.php?id=112396, August 22, 2006.
28. "Biological Overview," http://www.nti.org/e_research/profiles/India/Biological/print/index_2287.prt.
29. Charles D. Ferguson, "Assessing the Vulnerability of the Indian Civilian Nuclear

Program to Military and Terrorist Attack," in Henry Sokolski, ed., *Gauging US-Indian Strategic Cooperation,* March 2007, http://www.npec-web.org/Essays/20060913-Ferguson-AttacksOnFacilities.pdf

30. Rajesh M. Basrur and Hasan-Askari Rizvi, "Nuclear Terrorism and South Asia, Cooperative Monitoring," Center Occasional Paper No. 25, Sandia National Laboratories, SAND 98-0505/ February 25, 2003.
31. http://cisf.nic.in/
32. Ibid.
33. Arian L. Pregenzer, "Securing Nuclear Capabilities in India and Pakistan: Reducing the Terrorists and Proliferation Risks," http://cns.miis.edu/pubs/npr/vol10/101/101prege.pdf
34. Kishore Kuchibhotla and Matthew McKinzie, "Nuclear Terrorism and Nuclear Accidents in South Asia," http://www.stimson.org/southasia/pdf/reducingnukes-section5.pdf
35. Kuchibhotla and McKinzie, Ibid.
36. Adnan Gill, "How Secure is Indian Nuclear Programme," *The Pakistan Tribune,* October 17, 2006.
37. Rajesh Rajagopalan, *The Second Strike: Arguments About Nuclear War in South Asia* (Penguin Books India, 2005).
38. Ferguson, n. 29
39. B. Raman, "Al Qaeda's Shadow Over India?," *International Terrorism Monitor,* Paper no. 242, South Asia Analysis Group, http://www.saag.org/papers23/paper2267.html
40. David Albright, "Al Qaida's Nuclear Programme: Through the Window of Seized Documents," Nautilus Institute Special Forum 47, November 6, 2002, URL: www.nautilus.org/fora/special-Policy-Forum/47_Albright.html#sect2
41. The 9/11 Commission Report: Final Report of the National Commission on Terrorist Attacks Upon the United States, Official Government Edition (Washington, DC: US Government Printing Officc, 2004), URL: http://www.gpoasccess.gov/911/pdf/full-report.pdf, p. 172.
42. Electric Power Research Institute, "Deterring Terrorism: Aircraft Crash Impact Analyses Demonstrate Nuclear Power Plant's Structural Strength," Nuclear Energy Institute, December 2002.
43. Nuclear Control Institute, National Press Club Briefing, September 25, 2001, state-

ment by Edwin Lyman.

44. Department of Atomic Energy, "Nuclear India," July-August 2000, available at: http://www.dae.gov.in/ni/niju100/niju100.htm
45. "Indian Atomic Energy Body Wants 'No Fly Zones' Over Nuke Facilities," Deutsche Presse-Agentur, February 5, 2002, in Lexis-Nexis Academic Universe, February 13, 2005, http://www.lexis-nexis.com.
    http://www.nti.org/e_research/profiles/India/Nuclear/2296_5275.html
46. Ibid.
47. Quoted in Judith Vidal-Hall, "Naxalites," pp. 73–75, *Index on Censorship,* 35, no. 4, 2006, p. 74.
48. Vidal-Hall, Ibid.
49. "No Threat to Kaiga Nuclear Plant," http://naxalwatch.blogspot.com/2007/07/no-threat-to-kaiga-nuclear-plant.html, July 31, 2007.
50. Seema Mustafa, "Naxals Quietly Expand Base," *The Asian Age,* October 14, 2007.
51. Mark Thompson, "An Unstable Nation with WMD – and Extremists Who Would Die for Them. How Afraid Should We Be?," *Time,* January 18, 2008.
52. Statement by H.E. Mr. Tapan Choudhury, adviser (minister), Ministry of Science & Technology of Bangladesh at the 51st Session of General Conference of IAEA Vienna, September 17,2007, http://www.iaea.org/About/Policy/GC/GC51/Statements/bangladesh.pdf
53. Alex Stolar, "The Implications of Unrest in Pakistan for Nuclear Security," http://www.stimson.org/southasia/?SN=SA200705181263
54. "Testimony of Kamal Mitra Chenoy, US Commission on International Religious Freedom Hearing on Communal Violence in Gujarat, India and the US Response," June 10, 2002, http://coalitionagainstgenocide.org/reports/2002/uscirf.10jun2002.kamal.pdf
55. "Japan's Nuclear Leak: Earthquakes, Fire and Fault Lines," July 19, 2007, http://www.greenpeace.org.uk/blog/nuclear/japans-nuclear-leak-20070719
56. P.R. Chari, *Proliferation of Fissile Materials: The Indian Experience,* ACDIS Occasional Paper, University of Illinois at Urbana-Champaign, September 1998, p. 3.
57. Ferguson, n. 29.
58. National Report to the Convention on Nuclear Safety, Fourth Review Meeting of Contracting Parties, April 2008, Government of India, September 2007.

59. Manpreet Sethi, "Nuclear Security: Critical for Future Nuclear Expansion," *Air Power,* vol.1, no. 2, Winter 2006 p.110.
60. V.K. Shashikumar, "Leaks at India's Nuclear-Power Plants: Cause for Concern?," http://www.csmonitor.com/2002/1011/p07s01-wosc.html
61. Shashikumar, Ibid.
62. K.S. Jayaraman, "Head of Indian Nuclear Agency Loses Job After Going Critical," *Nature,* June 27, 1996.
63. http://www.mha.nic.in/acts-rules/The%20Explosive%20Substances%20Act,%201908.pdf
64. http://www.dae.gov.in/rules/aeact.htm
65. http://www.meaindia.nic.in/actsadm/30aa08.pdf
66. http://www.rajyasabha.nic.in/bills-ls-rs/2005/LV_2005.pdf
67. See Department of Atomic Energy, *Indian Atomic Programme: The First Ten Years,* Government of India, 1958.
68. *The Gazette of India,* Extraordinary, Part II-Section I, Reg. No. DL-(N)04/07/2003-05, New Delhi, June 2005.
69. SAARC Regional Convention on Suppression of Terrorism, http://untreaty.un.org/English/Terrorism/Conv18.pdf
70. Additional Protocol to the SAARC Regional Convention on Suppression of Terrorism, http://www.satp.org/satporgtp/southasia/documents/papers/SAARC_pak.htm
71. "On India's Accession to the Convention on the Physical Protection of Nuclear" Material, 1980, http://meaindia.nic.in/pressrelease/2002/01/22pr01.htm
72. Nuclear Terrorism: India Signs Convention, http://www.hindu.com/2006/07/26/stories/2006072607071200.htm
73. Mohammed El Baradei, "IAEA Director General Welcomes US and India Nuclear Deal," International Atomic Energy Agency Press Release 2006/05, March 2, 2006.
74. "Success Stories - Radiation Protection," http://www.barc.ernet.in/rcaindia/4_7.html
75. Information in this section is based on the conversation with an anonymous Indian nuclear scientist.
76. All information in this section is obtained from a discussion with an anonymous Indian nuclear scientist.
77. Pushparaja, K.S. Pradeepkumar, D.N. Sharma and H.S. Kushwaha, "Philosophy and Principles of Radiation Protection, Security of Radioactive Sources and Preparedness

for Response to Radiological Emergencies," http://www.barc.gov.in/publications/nl/2006/200612-1.pdf

78. n. 76.

79. Ibid.

80. Dhirendra Sharma, "India's N-Deterrence in Place?", http://www.greens-efa.org/cms/default/dokbin/171/171776.pdf

81. Sharma, Ibid.

82. http://www.barc.ernet.in/rcaindia/1_4.html

83. "India Cannot Cope with a Nuclear Attack," , http://www.rediff.com/news/2006/aug/22nuke.htm, August 22, 2006.

84. Statement by Congressman Adam Schiff, Hearing on H.R. 2631, Nuclear Forensics and Attribution Act House Committee on Homeland Security Subcommittee on Emerging Threats, Cybersecurity, and Science and Technology, October 10, 2007, http://homeland.house.gov/SiteDocuments/20071010175127-33681.pdf

Appendix I

United Nations
S/RES/1540 (2004)

Security Council
Distr.: General
28 April 2004

Resolution 1540 (2004)

Adopted by the Security Council at its 4956th meeting, on 28 April 2004

The Security Council,

Affirming that proliferation of nuclear, chemical and biological weapons, as well as their means of delivery,* constitutes a threat to international peace and security,

Reaffirming, in this context, the Statement of its President adopted at the Council's meeting at the level of Heads of State and Government on 31 January 1992 (S/23500), including the need for all Member States to fulfil their obligations in relation to arms control and disarmament and to prevent proliferation in all its aspects of all weapons of mass destruction,

Recalling also that the Statement underlined the need for all Member States to resolve peacefully in accordance with the Charter any problems in that context threatening or disrupting the maintenance of regional and global stability,

Affirming its resolve to take appropriate and effective actions against any threat to international peace and security caused by the proliferation of nuclear, chemical and biological weapons and their means of delivery, in conformity with its primary responsibilities, as provided for in the United Nations Charter,

* Definitions for the purpose of this resolution only: Means of delivery: missiles, rockets and other unmanned systems capable of delivering nuclear, chemical, or biological weapons, that are specially designed for such use. Non-State actor: individual or entity, not acting under the lawful authority of any State in conducting activities which come within the scope of this resolution. Related materials: materials, equipment and technology covered by relevant multilateral treaties and arrangements, or included on national control lists, which could be used for the design, development, production or use of nuclear, chemical and biological weapons and their means of delivery.

Affirming its support for the multilateral treaties whose aim is to eliminate or prevent the proliferation of nuclear, chemical or biological weapons and the importance for all States parties to these treaties to implement them fully in order to promote international stability,

Welcoming efforts in this context by multilateral arrangements which contribute to non-proliferation,

Affirming that prevention of proliferation of nuclear, chemical and biological weapons should not hamper international cooperation in materials, equipment and technology for peaceful purposes while goals of peaceful utilization should not be used as a cover for proliferation,

Gravely concerned by the threat of terrorism and the risk that non-State actors* such as those identified in the United Nations list established and maintained by the Committee established under Security Council resolution 1267 and those to whom resolution 1373 applies, may acquire, develop, traffic in or use nuclear, chemical and biological weapons and their means of delivery,

Gravely concerned by the threat of illicit trafficking in nuclear, chemical, or biological weapons and their means of delivery, and related materials,* which adds a new dimension to the issue of proliferation of such weapons and also poses a threat to international peace and security,

Recognizing the need to enhance coordination of efforts on national, subregional, regional and international levels in order to strengthen a global response to this serious challenge and threat to international security,

Recognizing that most States have undertaken binding legal obligations under treaties to which they are parties, or have made other commitments aimed at preventing the proliferation of nuclear, chemical or biological weapons, and have taken effective measures to account for, secure and physically protect sensitive materials, such as those required by the Convention on the Physical Protection of Nuclear Materials and those recommended by the IAEA Code of Conduct on the Safety and Security of Radioactive Sources,

Recognizing further the urgent need for all States to take additional effective measures to prevent the proliferation of nuclear, chemical or biological weapons and their means of delivery,

APPENDIX I

Encouraging all Member States to implement fully the disarmament treaties and agreements to which they are party,

Reaffirming the need to combat by all means, in accordance with the Charter of the United Nations, threats to international peace and security caused by terrorist acts,

Determined to facilitate henceforth an effective response to global threats in the area of non-proliferation,

Acting under Chapter VII of the Charter of the United Nations,

1. *Decides* that all States shall refrain from providing any form of support to non-State actors that attempt to develop, acquire, manufacture, possess, transport, transfer or use nuclear, chemical or biological weapons and their means of delivery;
2. *Decides* also that all States, in accordance with their national procedures, shall adopt and enforce appropriate effective laws which prohibit any non-State actor to manufacture, acquire, possess, develop, transport, transfer or use nuclear, chemical or biological weapons and their means of delivery, in particular for terrorist purposes, as well as attempts to engage in any of the foregoing activities, participate in them as an accomplice, assist or finance them;
3. *Decides* also that all States shall take and enforce effective measures to establish domestic controls to prevent the proliferation of nuclear, chemical, or biological weapons and their means of delivery, including by establishing appropriate controls over related materials and to this end shall:
   (a) Develop and maintain appropriate effective measures to account for and secure such items in production, use, storage or transport;
   (b) Develop and maintain appropriate effective physical protection measures;
   (c) Develop and maintain appropriate effective border controls and law enforcement efforts to detect, deter, prevent and combat, including through international cooperation when necessary, the illicit trafficking and brokering in such items in accordance with their national legal authorities and legislation and consistent with international law;

(d) Establish, develop, review and maintain appropriate effective national export and trans-shipment controls over such items, including appropriate laws and regulations to control export, transit, trans-shipment and re-export and controls on providing funds and services related to such export and trans-shipment such as financing, and transporting that would contribute to proliferation, as well as establishing end-user controls; and establishing and enforcing appropriate criminal or civil penalties for violations of such export control laws and regulations;

4. *Decides* to establish, in accordance with rule 28 of its provisional rules of procedure, for a period of no longer than two years, a Committee of the Security Council, consisting of all members of the Council, which will, calling as appropriate on other expertise, report to the Security Council for its examination, on the implementation of this resolution, and to this end calls upon States to present a first report no later than six months from the adoption of this resolution to the Committee on steps they have taken or intend to take to implement this resolution;
5. *Decides* that none of the obligations set forth in this resolution shall be interpreted so as to conflict with or alter the rights and obligations of State Parties to the Nuclear Non-Proliferation Treaty, the Chemical Weapons Convention and the Biological and Toxin Weapons Convention or alter the responsibilities of the International Atomic Energy Agency or the Organization for the Prohibition of Chemical Weapons;
6. *Recognizes* the utility in implementing this resolution of effective national control lists and calls upon all Member States, when necessary, to pursue at the earliest opportunity the development of such lists;
7. *Recognizes* that some States may require assistance in implementing the provisions of this resolution within their territories and invites States in a position to do so to offer assistance as appropriate in response to specific requests to the States lacking the legal and regulatory infrastructure, implementation experience and/or resources for fulfilling the above provisions;
8. *Calls* upon all States:

(a) To promote the universal adoption and full implementation, and, where necessary, strengthening of multilateral treaties to which they are parties, whose aim is to prevent the proliferation of nuclear, biological or chemical weapons;

(b) To adopt national rules and regulations, where it has not yet been done, to ensure compliance with their commitments under the key multilateral nonproliferation treaties;

(c) To renew and fulfil their commitment to multilateral cooperation, in particular within the framework of the International Atomic Energy Agency, the Organization for the Prohibition of Chemical Weapons and the Biological and Toxin Weapons Convention, as important means of pursuing and achieving their common objectives in the area of non-proliferation and of promoting international cooperation for peaceful purposes;

(d) To develop appropriate ways to work with and inform industry and the public regarding their obligations under such laws;

9. *Calls* upon all States to promote dialogue and cooperation on nonproliferation so as to address the threat posed by proliferation of nuclear, chemical, or biological weapons, and their means of delivery;

10. Further to counter that threat, *calls* upon all States, in accordance with their national legal authorities and legislation and consistent with international law, to take cooperative action to prevent illicit trafficking in nuclear, chemical or biological weapons, their means of delivery, and related materials;

11. *Expresses* its intention to monitor closely the implementation of this resolution and, at the appropriate level, to take further decisions which may be required to this end;

12. *Decides* to remain seized of the matter.

Appendix II

Convention on the Physical Protection of Nuclear Material (CPPNM)

The States Parties to this Convention
Recognizing the right of all States to develop and apply nuclear energy for peaceful purposes and their legitimate interests in the potential benefits to be derived from the peaceful application of nuclear energy;

Convinced of the need for facilitating international cooperation in the peaceful application of nuclear energy;

Desiring to avert the potential dangers posed by the unlawful taking and use of nuclear material;

Convinced that offences relating to nuclear material are a matter of grave concern and that there is an urgent need to adopt appropriate and effective measures to ensure the prevention, detection and punishment of such offences;

Aware of the need for international cooperation to establish, in conformity with the national law of each State Party and with this Convention, effective measures for the physical protection of nuclear material;

Convinced that this Convention should facilitate the safe transfer of nuclear material;

Stressing also the importance of the physical protection of nuclear material in domestic use, storage and transport;

Recognizing the importance of effective physical protection of nuclear material used for military purposes, and understanding that such material is and will continue to be accorded stringent physical protection;

Have agreed as follows:

Article 1

For the purposes of this Convention:

a. "nuclear material" means plutonium except that with isotopic concentration exceeding 80% in plutonium-238; uranium-233; uranium enriched in the isotope 235 or 233; uranium containing the mixture of isotopes as occurring in nature other than in the form of ore or ore-residue; any material containing one or more of the foregoing;

b. "uranium enriched in the isotope 235 or 233" means uranium containing the isotope 235 or 233 or both in an amount such that the abundance ratio of the sum of these isotopes to the isotope 238 is greater than the ratio of the isotope 235 to the isotope 238 occurring in nature;

c. "international nuclear transport" means the carriage of a consignment of nuclear material by any means of transportation intended to go beyond the territory of the State where the shipment originates beginning with the departure from a facility of the shipper in that State and ending with the arrival at a facility of the receiver within the State of ultimate destination.

Article 2

1. This Convention shall apply to nuclear material used for peaceful purposes while in international nuclear transport.
2. With the exception of Articles 3 and 4 and paragraph 3 of Article 5, this Convention shall also apply to nuclear material used for peaceful purposes while in domestic use, storage and transport.
3. Apart from the commitments expressly undertaken by States Parties in the articles covered by paragraph 2 with respect to nuclear material used for peaceful purposes while in domestic use, storage and transport, nothing in this Convention shall be interpreted as affecting the sovereign rights of a State regarding the domestic use, storage and transport of such nuclear material.

Article 3

Each State Party shall take appropriate steps within the framework of its national law and consistent with international law to ensure as far as practicable that, during international nuclear transport, nuclear material within its territory, or on board a ship or aircraft under its jurisdiction insofar as such ship or aircraft is engaged in the transport to or from that State, is protected at the levels described in Annex I.

Article 4

1. Each State Party shall not export or authorize the export of nuclear material unless the State Party has received assurances that such material will be protected during the interrogational nuclear transport at the levels described in Annex I.
2. Each State Party shall not import or authorize the import of nuclear material from a State not party to this Convention unless the State Party has received assurances that such material will during the interrogational nuclear transport be protected at the levels described in Annex I.
3. A State Party shall not allow the transit of its territory by land or internal waterways or through its airports or seaports of nuclear material between states that are not parties to this Convention unless the State Party has received assurances as far as practicable that this nuclear material will be protected during international nuclear transport at the levels described in Annex I.
4. Each State Party shall apply with the framework of its national law the levels of physical protection described in Annex I to nuclear material being transported from a part of that State to another part of the same State through international waters or airspace.
5. The State Party responsible for receiving assurances that the nuclear material will be protected at the levels described in Annex I according to paragraphs 1 to 3 shall identify and inform in advance States which the nuclear material is expected to transit by land or internal waterways, or whose airports or seaports it is expected to enter.
6. The responsibility for obtaining assurances referred to in paragraph 1 may be transferred, by mutual agreement, to the State Party involved in the transport as the importing State.
7. Nothing in this Article shall be interpreted as in any way affecting the territorial sovereignty and jurisdiction of a State, including that over its airspace and territorial sea.

Article 5

1. States Parties shall identify and make known to each other directly or through the International Atomic Energy Agency their central authority and point of contact having responsibility for physical protection of nuclear material and for coordinating recovery and response operations in the event of any unauthorized removal, use or alteration of nuclear material or in the event of credible threat thereof.
2. In the case of theft, robbery or any other unlawful taking of nuclear material or of credible threat thereof, States Parties shall, in accordance with their national law, provide cooperation and assistance to the maximum feasible extent in the recovery and protection of such material to any State that so requests. In particular:
   a. a State Party shall take appropriate steps to inform as soon as possible other States, which appear to it to be concerned, of any theft, robbery or other unlawful taking of nuclear material or credible threat thereof and to inform, where appropriate, international organizations;
   b. as appropriate, the States Parties concerned shall exchange information of threatened nuclear material, verifying the integrity of the shipping container, or recovering unlawfully taken nuclear material and shall:
      i. Coordinate their efforts through diplomatic and other agreed channels;
      ii. Render assistance; if requested;
      iii. Ensure the return of nuclear material stolen or missing as a consequence of the above-mentioned events.

   The means of implementation of this cooperation shall be determined by the States Parties concerned.
3. States Parties shall cooperate and consult as appropriate, with each other directly or through international organizations, with a view to obtaining guidance on the design, maintenance and improvement of systems of physical protection of nuclear material in international transport.

Article 6

1. State Parties shall take appropriate measures consistent with their national law to protect the confidentiality of any information which they receive in

confidence by virtue of the provisions of this Convention from another State Party or through participation in an activity carried out for the implementation of this Convention. If States Parties provide information to international organizations in confidence, steps shall be taken to ensure that the confidentiality of such information is protected.

2. States Parties shall not be required by this Convention to provide any information which they are not permitted to communicate pursuant to national law or which would jeopardize the security of the State concerned or the physical protection of nuclear material.

Article 7

1. The intentional commission of:
   a. an act without lawful authority which constitutes the receipt, possession, use, transfer, alteration, disposal or dispersal of nuclear material and which causes or is likely to cause death or serious injury to any person or substantial damage to property;
   b. a theft or robbery of nuclear material;
   c. an embezzlement or fraudulent obtaining of nuclear material;
   d. an act constituting a demand for nuclear material by threat or use of force or by any other form of intimidation;
   e. a threat:
      i. to use nuclear material to cause death or serious injury to any person or substantial property damage, or
      ii. to commit an offence described in sub-paragraph (b) in order to compel a natural or legal person, international organization or State to do or to refrain from doing any act;
   f. an attempt to commit any offence described in paragraphs (a), (b) or (c); and
   g. an act which constitutes participation in any offence described in paragraphs (a) to (f)

   shall be made a punishable offence by each State Party under its national law.
2. Each State Party shall make the offences described in this Article punishable by appropriate penalties which take into account their grave nature.

Article 8

1. Each State Party shall take such measures as may be necessary to establish its jurisdiction over the offences set forth in Article 7 in the following cases;
   a. when the offence is committed in the territory of that State or on board a ship or aircraft registered in that State;
   b. when the alleged offender is a national of that State.
2. Each State Party shall likewise take such measures as may be necessary to establish its jurisdiction over these offences in cases where the alleged offender is present in its territory and it does not extradite him pursuant to Article 11 to any of the States mentioned in paragraph 1.
3. This Convention does not exclude any criminal jurisdiction exercised in accordance with national law.
4. In addition to the States Parties mentioned in paragraphs 1 and 2, each State Party may, consistent with international law, establish its jurisdiction over the offences set forth in Article 7 when it is involved in international nuclear transport as the exporting or importing State.

Article 9

Upon being satisfied that the circumstances so warrant, the State Party in whose territory the alleged offender is present, shall take appropriate measures, including detention, under its national law to ensure his presence for the purpose of prosecution or extradition. Measures taken according to this Article shall be notified without delay to the States required to establish jurisdiction pursuant to Article 8 and, where appropriate, all other States concerned.

Article 10

The State Party in whose territory the alleged offender is present shall, if it does not extradite him, submit, without exception whatsoever and without undue delay, the case to its competent authorities for the purpose of prosecution, through proceedings in accordance with the laws of that State.

Article 11

1. The offences in Article 7 shall be deemed to be included as extraditable

offences in any extradition treaty existing between States Parties. States Parties undertake to include those offences as extraditable offences in every future extradition treaty to be concluded between them.

2. If a State Party which makes extradition conditional on the existence of a treaty receives a request for extradition from another State Party with which it has no extradition treaty, it may as its option consider this Convention as the legal basis for extradition in respect of those offences. Extradition shall be subject to the other conditions provided by the law of the requested State.
3. States Parties which do not make extradition conditional on the existence of a treaty shall recognize those offences as extraditable offences between themselves subject to the conditions provided by the law of the requested State.
4. Each of the offences shall be treated, for the purpose of extradition between States Parties, as if it had been committed not only in the place in which it occurred but also in the territories of the States Parties required to establish their jurisdiction in accordance with paragraph 1 of Article 8.

Article 12

Any person regarding whom proceedings are being carried out in connection with any of the offences set forth in Article 7 shall be guaranteed fair treatment at all stages of the proceedings.

Article 13

1. States Parties shall afford one another the greatest measure of assistance in connection with criminal proceedings brought in respect of the offences set forth in Article 7, including the supply of evidence at their disposal necessary for the proceedings. The law of the State requested shall apply in all cases.
2. The provisions of paragraph I shall not affect obligations under any other treaty, bilateral or multilateral, which governs or will govern, in whole or in part, mutual assistance in criminal matters.

Article 14

1. Each State Party shall inform the depositary of its law and regulations which give effect to this Convention. The depositary shall communicate such information periodically to all State Parties.
2. The State Party where an alleged offender is prosecuted shall, wherever practicable, first communicate the final outcome of the proceedings to the State directly concerned. The State Party shall also communicate the final outcome to the depositary who shall inform all States.
3. Where an offence involves nuclear material used for peaceful purposes in domestic use, storage or transport and both the alleged offender and the nuclear material remain in the territory of the State Party in which the offence was committed, nothing in this Convention shall be interpreted as requiring that State Party to provide information concerning criminal proceedings arising out of such an offence.

Article 15

The Annexes constitute an integral part of this Convention.

Article 16

1. A conference of States Parties shall be convened by the depositary five years after the entry into force of this Convention to review the implementation of the Convention and its adequacy as concerns the preamble, the whole of the operative part and the annexes in the light of the then prevailing situation.
2. At intervals of not less than five years thereafter, the majority of States Parties may obtain, by submitting a proposal to this effect to the depositary, the convening of further conferences with the same objective.

Article 17

1. In the event of a dispute between two or more States Parties concerning the interpretation or application of this Convention, such States Parties shall consult with a view to the settlement of the dispute by negotiation, or by any other peaceful means of settling disputes acceptable to all parties to the dispute.

2. Any dispute of this character which cannot be settled in the manner prescribed in paragraph 1 shall, at the request of any party to such dispute, be submitted to arbitration or referred to the International Court of Justice for decision. Where a dispute is submitted to arbitration, if, within six months from the date of the request, the parties to the dispute are unable to agree on the organization of the arbitration, a party may request the President of the International Court of Justice or the Secretary-General of the United Nations to appoint one or more arbitrators. In case of conflicting requests by the parties to the dispute, the request to the Secretary-General of the United Nations shall have priority.
3. Each State Party may, at the time of signature, ratification, acceptance or approval of this Convention or accession thereto, declare that it does not consider itself bound by either or both of the dispute settlement procedures provided for in paragraph 2. The other State Parties shall not be bound by a dispute settlement procedure provided for in paragraph 2, with respect to a State Party which has made a reservation to that procedure.
4. Any State Party which has made a reservation in accordance with paragraph 3 may at any time withdraw that reservation by notification to the depositary.

Article 18

1. This Convention shall be open for signature by all States at the Headquarters of the International Atomic Energy Agency in Vienna and at the Headquarters of the United Nations in New York from 3 March 1980 until its entry into force.
2. This Convention is subject to ratification, acceptance or approval by the signatory States.
3. After its entry into force, this Convention will be open for accession by all States.
4.
   a. This Convention shall be open for signature or accession by international organizations and regional organizations of an integration or other nature, provided that any such organization is constituted by

sovereign States and has competence in respect of the negotiation, conclusion and application of international agreements in matters covered by this Convention.

b. In matters within their competence, such organizations shall, on their own behalf, exercise the rights and fulfil the responsibilities which this Convention attributes to State Parties.
c. When becoming party to this Convention, such an organization shall communicate to the depository a declaration indicating which States are members thereof and which Articles of this Convention do not apply to it.
d. Such an organization shall not hold any vote additional to those of its Member States.

5. Instruments of ratification, acceptance, approval or accession shall be deposited with depositary.

Article 19

1. This Convention shall enter into force on the thirtieth day following the date of deposit of the twenty-first instrument of ratification, acceptance or approval with depositary.
2. For each State ratifying, accepting approving or acceding to the Convention after the date of deposit of the twenty-first instrument of ratification, acceptance or approval, the Convention shall enter into force on the thirtieth day after deposit by such State of its instrument of its instrument of ratification, acceptance, approval or accession.

Article 20

1. Without prejudice to Article 16, a State Party may propose amendments to this Convention. The proposed amendment shall be submitted to the depositary who shall circulate it immediately to all States Parties. If a majority of States Parties request the depositary to convene a conference to consider the proposed amendments, the depositary shall invite all States Parties to attend such a conference being not sooner than thirty days after the invitations are issued. Any amendment adopted at the

conference by a two-thirds majority of all State Parties shall be promptly circulated by the depositary to all States Parties.

2. The amendment shall enter into force for each State Party that deposits its Instrument of ratification, acceptance or approval of the amendment on the thirtieth day after the date on which two-thirds of the State Parties have deposited their instruments of ratification, acceptance or approval with the depositary. Thereafter, the amendement shall enter into force for any other State Party on the day on which that State Party deposits its instrument of ratification, acceptance or approval of the amendment.

Article 21

1. Any State Party may denounce this Convention by written notification to the depositary.
2. Denunciation shall take effect one hundred and eighty days following the date on which notification is received by the depositary.

Article 22

The depositary shall promptly notify all States of:

a. each signature of this Convention;
b. each deposit of an instrument of ratification, acceptance, approval or accession;
c. any reservation or withdrawal in accordance with Article 17;
d. any communication made by an organization in accordance with paragraph 4(c)of Article 18;
e. the entry into force of this Convention;
f. the entry into force of any amendment to this Convention; and
g. any denunciation made under Article 21.

Article 23

The original of this Convention, of which the Arabic, Chinese, English, French, Russian and Spanish texts are equally authentic, shall be deposited with the Director General of the International Atomic Energy Agency who shall send certified copies thereof to all States.

IN WITNESS WHEREOF, the undersigned, being duly authorized, have signed this Convention, opened for signature at Vienna and at New York on March 3, 1980.

Annex 1

Levels of Physical Protection to be Applied in International Transport of Nuclear Materials as Categorized in Annex II

1. Levels of physical protection for nuclear material during storage incidental to international nuclear transport include:
   a. For Category III materials, storage within an area to which access is controlled;
   b. For Category II materials, storage within an area under constant surveillance by guards or electronic devices, surrounded by a physical barrier with a limited number of points of entry under appropriate control or any area with an equivalent level of physical protection;
   c. For Category I materials, storage within a protected area as defined for Category II above, to which ,in addition, access is restricted to persons whose trustworthiness has been determined, and which is under surveillance by guards who are in close communication with appropriate response forces. Specific measures taken in this context should have as their object the detection and prevention of any assault, unauthorized access or unauthorized removal of material.
2. Levels of physical protection for nuclear material during international transport include:

   For Category II and III materials, transportation shall take place under special precautions including prior arrangements among sender, receiver, and carrier, and prior agreement between natural or legal persons subject to the jurisdiction and regulations of exporting and importing States, specifying time, place and procedures for transferring transport responsibility;

a. For Category I materials, transportation shall take place under special precautions identified above for transportation of Category II and III materials, and in addition, under constant surveillance by escorts and under conditions which assure close communication with appropriate response forces;

b. For natural uranium other than in the form of ore or ore-residue; transportation protection for quantities exceeding 500 kilograms uranium shall include advance notification of shipment specifying mode of transport, expected time of arrival and confirmation of receipt of shipment.

Annex II

Table: Categorization of Nuclear Material

Material	Form	Category		
		I	II	III
1.Plutonium	Unirradiated[b/]	2 kg or more	Less than 2 kg but more than 500 g	500 g or less but more than 15 g
2. Uranium[235]	Unirradiated[b/] • uranium enriched to 20 % 235U or more • uranium enriched to10% ^{235}U but less than 20% • uranium enriched to 10% 235U	5 kg or more	Less than 5 kg but more than 1kg 10kg or more	1kg or less but more than 15 g Less than 10 kg but more than 1 kg
3. Uranium 233	Unirradiated[b/]	2 kg or more	Less than 2 kg but more than 500 kg	500g or less but more than 15 g
4. Irradiated fuel			Depleted or natural uranium, thorium or low-enriched fuel (less than 10 % fissile content)d/e/	

[a/] All plutonium except that with isotopic concentration exceeding 80% in plutonium-238.

[b/] Material not irradiated in a reactor or material irradiated in a reactor but with a radiation level equal to or less than 100 rads/hour at one metr unshielded.

[c/] Quantities not falling in Category III and natural uranium should be protected in accordance with prudent management practice.

d/ Although this level of protection is recommended, it would be open to States, upon evaluation of the specific circumstances, to assign a different category of physical protection.

e/ Other fuel which by virtue of its original fissile material content is classified as Category I and II before irradiation may be reduced one category level while the radiation level from the fuel exceeds 100 rads/hour at one metre unshielded.

Final Act

Meeting of Governmental Representatives to Consider the Drafting of a Convention on the Physical Protection of Nuclear Material

1. The Meeting of Governmental Representatives to Consider the Drafting of a Convention on the Physical Protection of Nuclear Material met in Vienna at the Headquarters of the International Atomic Energy Agency from 31 October to 10 November 1977, from 10 to 20 April 1978, from 5 to 16 February and from 15 to 26 October 1979. Informal consultations between Governmental Representatives took place from 4 to 7 September 1978 and from 24 to 25 September 1979.
2. Representatives of 58 States and one organization participated, namely, representatives of:

Algeria	Korea, Republic of
Argentina	Libyan Arab Jamahiriya
Australia	Luxembourg
Austria	Mexico
Belgium	Netherlands
Brazil	Niger
Bulgaria	Norway
Canada	Pakistan
Chile	Panama
Colombia	Paraguay

Costa Rica	Peru
Cuba	Philippines
Czechoslovakia	Poland
Denmark	Qatar
Ecuador	Romania
Egypt	South Africa
Finland	Spain
France	Sweden
German Democratic Republic	Switzerland
Germany, Federal Republic of	Tunisia
Greece	Turkey
Guatemala	Union of Soviet Socialist Republics
Holy See	United Arab Emirates
Hungary	United Kingdom of Great Britain and Northern Ireland
India	United States of America
Indonesia	Venezuela
Ireland	Yugoslavia
Israel	Zaire
Italy	European Atomic Energy Community
Japan	

3. The Following States and international organization participated as observers: Iran Lebanon, Malaysia, Thailand, Nuclear Energy Agency of the Organization for Economic Cooperation and Development
4. The Meeting elected Ambassador D.L. Siazon Jr. (Philippines) as Chairman. For the meetings in April 1978 and February 1979 Mr. R.A. Estrada-Oyuela (Argentina) was elected Chairman.
5. The Meeting elected as Vice-Chairmen:

Mr. K. Willuhn of the German Democratic Republic, who at the meeting in

February 1979 was succeeded by Mr. H. Rabold of the German Democratic Republic;

Mr. R.J.S. Harry, Netherlands, who at the meeting of October 1979 was succeeded by Mr. G. Dahlhoff of the Federal Republic of Germany;

Mr. R.A. Estrada-Qyuela, Argentina, who at the meeting of October 1979 was succeeded by Mr. L.A. Oiliveri of Argentina.

Mr. L.W. Herron (Australia) was elected Rapporteur. For the meeting in October 1979, Mr. N.R. Smith (Australia) was elected Rapporteur.

6. Secretariat services were provided by the International Atomic Energy Agency. The Director General of the Agency was represented by the Director of the Legal Division of the Agency, Mr. D.M. Edwards and, in succession to him, Mr. L.W. Herron.
7. The Meeting set up the following groups:
   a. Working Group on Technical Issues
      Chairman: Mr. R.J.S. Harry, Netherlands
   b. Working Group on Legal Issues
      Chairman: Mr. R.A. Estrada-Oyuela, Argentina
   c. Working Group on Scope of Convention
      Chairman: Mr. K. Willuhn, German Democratic Republic
   d. Drafting Committee
      Chairman: Mr. De Castro Neves, Brazil

   Members: Respresentatives of Australia, Brazil, Canada, Chile, Czechoslovakia, Eqypt, France, Federal Republic of Germany, Italy, Japan, Mexico, Qatar, Tunisia, Union of Soviet Socialist Republics, United States of America.
8. The Meeting had before it the following documents:
   Draft Convention on the Physical Protection of Nuclear Materials, Facilities and Transports, as contained in document CPNM/1;
   a. IAEA document INFCIR/225/Rev.1: The Physical Protection of Nuclear Material;

b. IAEA document INFCIRC/254: Communications Received from Certain Member States regarding Guidelines for the Export of Nuclear Material, Equipment or Technology.

9. The Meeting completed consideration of a Convention, the text of which is attached as Annex 1*. Certain delegations expressed reservations with regard to particular provisions in the text. These are recorded in the documents and in the Daily Reports of the Meeting. It was agreed that the text will be referred by delegations to their authorities for consideration.

10. The Meeting recommended that the text of the Convention be transmitted for information to the twenty-third General Conference of the International Atomic Energy Agency.

11. The Convention will, in accordance with its terms, be opened for signature from 3 March 1980 at the Headquarters of the International Atomic Energy Agency in Vienna and at the Headquarters of the United Nations in New York.

Vienna, 26 October 1979

(Signed)
D.L.Siazon Jr.

1. The text of the Convention was transmitted to the twenty-third (1979) regular session of the General Conference of the International Atomic Energy Agency, pursuant to paragraph 11 of the Final Act, as document INFCIRC/274.

* Since the Convention has been opened for signature, it is not attached here as Annex I; it is reproduced as the first part of this document.

Appendix III

US-Russian Agreement on Management of Used Plutonium

Agreement between the Government of the United States of America and the Government of the Russian Federation on Scientific and Technical Cooperation in the Management of Plutonium that has been withdrawn from Nuclear Military Programs

The Government of the United States of America and the Government of the Russian Federation, hereafter referred to as the Parties,

Taking into account:

(a) The January 14, 1994, Declaration of the Presidents of the United States and the Russian Federation on "Non-proliferation of Weapons of Mass Destruction and the Means of their Delivery";

(b) The Declaration of the April 19-20, 1996, Summit on Nuclear Safety and Security in Moscow;

(c) The Conclusions of the International Meeting of Experts in Paris, on October 28-31, 1996, concerning the safe and efficient management of fissile materials designated as no longer required for defense purposes;

(d) The statement regarding fissile materials in the June 22, 1997, Final Communiqué of the Denver Summit of the Eight;

(e) The statement of the President of the United States on March 1, 1995, that 200 tonnes of fissile material will be withdrawn from the US nuclear stockpile and directing that these materials will never again be used to build a nuclear weapon; and

(f) The message of the President of the Russian Federation to the participants of the 41st General Conference of the IAEA, September 26, 1997, on step-by-step removal from nuclear defense programs of up to 500 tonnes of highly enriched uranium and up to 50 tonnes of plutonium released in the process of nuclear disarmament;

Have agreed as follows:

Article 1

The purposes of this agreement are to:

(a) Provide the scientific and technical basis for decisions on how plutonium, subject to this agreement, shall be managed, and

(b) Establish a framework for continued and expanded scientific and technical cooperation for the accomplishment of the objective in paragraph A.

Article 2

For purposes of this agreement:

1. "Plutionium" means plutonium that has been withdrawn from nuclear military programs and is no longer required for defense purposes.
2. "Management of plutonium" means the transformation of plutonium into spent fuel or other forms equally unusable for nuclear weapons or other nuclear explosive devices, and may include conversion of plutonium and its manufacture into MOX fuel, use of MOX fuel in nuclear reactors, and immobilization of plutonium in various form.

Article 3

1. The Parties shall:
   (a) Continue to cooperate with small-scale tests and demonstrations relating to management to plutonium; and
   (b) As soon as is practicable, also proceed to pilot-scale demonstrations of technologies for plutonium management.
2. The principal subject areas for the Parties' cooperative efforts shall be:
   (a) Conversion of metallic plutonium into oxide suitable for the manufacture of MOX fuel for nuclear power reactors of various types;
   (b) Stabilization of unstable forms of plutonium;
   (c) Use of plutonium in the form of MOX fuel in various types of nuclear power reactors;
   (d) Immobilization of plutonium, including wastes and hard-to –process forms; and

(e) Disposal of immobilized forms of materials containing plutonium in deep geological formations.

Article 4

1. The Parties shall designate executive agents to carry out the provisions of this agreement. The executive agent for the United States of America shall be the US Department of Energy and the executive agent for the Russian Federation shall be the Russian Ministry for Atomic Energy.
2. The Parties shall have the right, consistent with their respective laws and regulations, and following written notification to the other Party, to obtain participation, as necessary, in the implementation of this agreement, by other agencies, departments, and units of their respective governments
3. To accomplish the objectives of this agreement, the Parties shall establish a US-Russian joint steering committee on plutonium management, which shall coordinate and agree upon work undertaken under this agreement. Each Party shall designate its members on the joint steering committee. Decisions of the joint steering committee shall be taken by consensus.
4. The tasks of the join steering committee shall include:
   (a) Development of overall work programs and areas of cooperation within the scope of this agreement;
   (b) Prioritization, coordination, review and approval of the cooperative projects under this agreement with the resources made available by the parties;
   (c) Resolution of any disputes that may arise with respect to the scientific and technical work performed under this agreement; and
   (d) Such other matters, as the Parties may agree, that are within the scope of this agreement.
5. When agreement is reached on the performance of joint research, projects, or experiments under this agreement, detailed procedures for performing the activities involved shall be officially drawn up in the form of implementing arrangements, to be reviewed and approved by the joint steering committee.

Article 5

Cooperation between the parties within the framework of this agreement may include the following:

(a) Sharing of scientific and technical information;

(b) Development of conceptual approaches;

(c) Research, experiments and small-scale demonstrations of technological solutions;

(d) Design, construction, and operation of pilot-scale facilities for demonstrating and testing technological solutions obtained as a result or research;

(e) Transfer of equipment and non-nuclear materials;

(f) Meetings, seminars, conferences, personnel assignment, and workshops for the sharing of information;

(g) Feasibility studies; and

(h) Such other forms of cooperation within the scope of this agreement as the executive agents may agree upon in writing.

Article 6

1. In the implementation of this agreement, only unclassified information shall be exchanged.
2. In order to prevent access to it by people and organizations not participating in the implementation of this agreement, information provided by the Parties pursuant to, or produced as a result of, this agreement which is considered sensitive by the Parties is to be held in confidence and must be clearly designate and marked. The Party transmitting the information will designate information as sensitive in accordance with its internal laws and regulations. The party receiving this information shall assign it a designation that provides a degree of protection at least equivalent to that required by the Party that furnished the information.
3. Sensitive information shall be handled in accordance with the laws and regulations of the Party receiving the information, and shall not be disclosed or transmitted to a third party not participating in implementation of this agreement without the written consent of the Party transmitting the

information. According to the regulations of the United States, such information shall be treated as foreign government information provided in confidence and shall be protected appropriately. According to the norms and regulations of the Russian Federation, such information shall be treated as official information with limited distribution and shall be protected appropriately.

4. The Parties shall assure effective protection and allocation of rights to intellectual property transmitted or created under this agreement, as set forth in this Article and in the annex to this agreement, which forms an integral part of this agreement.
5. Information transmitted under this agreement must be used solely in accordance with this agreement.
6. The number of people having access to sensitive information must be limited to the number necessary to implement this agreement and other programs associated with this agreement, and shall be determined by the Parties' executive agents.

Article 7

1. Materials, equipment and technologies, transferred under the terms of this agreement, shall not be used for the production of nuclear weapons, any nuclear explosive devices, or for research or development of such devices or for the furtherance of any military purpose.
2. Materials, equipment and technologies, transferred under the terms of this agreement, shall not be exported, re-exported, or transferred from the Jurisdiction of the recipient without the written consent of the Parties.
3. Prior to the export under the terms of this agreement to a third party of any equipment, materials or technologies, the Parties by mutual agreement in writing shall define the conditions in accordance with which such items shall be exported, re-exported, or transferred from the jurisdiction of the third party.
4. The Parties' executive agents shall take all measures necessary to ensure adequate physical protection of nuclear materials, equipment, installations, and nuclear technologies in its jurisdiction, and shall apply criteria and

levels of physical protection of nuclear material and in recommendations of the iaea.

Article 8

Equipment, supplies, materials, services and activities provided or acquired by the United States of America ,its contractors, subcontractors, and their personnel for the implementation of this agreement are free technical assistance and are thus exempt from customs duties and taxes The Russian Federation shall take all necessary measures to exempt this equipment, shipment, materials, services, and work from all taxes, tariffs, customs duties, and levies of the Russian Federation and its instrumentalities

Article 9

1. With the exception of claims for damage or injury against individuals arising from their premeditated actions, the Government of the Russian Federation shall bring no claim or other legal proceedings against the Government of the United States of America and its personnel or its contractors, sub-contractors, consultants, suppliers or subsuppliers of equipment or services at any tier and their personnel, in any court or forum, for any damage, including indirect, direct or consequential damage, arising from activities undertaken pursuant to this agreement, to property owned by the Russian Federation. This paragraph shall not apply to legal actions brought by the Government of the Russian Fedration to enforce the provisions of contracts to which it or a Russian national or other legal entity is a party.
2. With the exception of claims for damage or injury against individuals arising from their premeditated actions, the Government of the Russian Federation shall provide for the adequate defense of, shall indemnify, and shall bring no claims or other legal proceedings against, the Government of the United States of America and its personnel or its contactors, subcontractors, consultants, suppliers or subsuppliers of equipment or services at any tier and their personnel, in connection with third-party claims, in any court or forum, for any injury or damage, including indirect, direct, or consequential injury or damage, arising from activities undertaken pursuant to this agreement,

occurring within or outside the territory of the Russian Federation. Nothing in this paragraph shall be construed as acknowledging the jurisdiction of any court or forum over third-party claims to which this paragraph applies, nor shall it be construed as waiving the sovereign immunity of either Party with respect to third-party claims that may be brought against it.

3. The Parties may, as necessary, conduct consultations regarding claim and legal proceedings concerning this article.
4. The provisions of this Article shall not prevent the Parties from providing compensation in accordance with their national laws.
5. Nothing in this Article shall be interpreted to prevent legal proceedings or claims against nationals of the Russian Federation or permanent residents of the Russian Federation.

Article 10

1. Join activities under this agreement shall be supported by funds and in-kind contribution of equipment, material, and labor provided on a non-reimbursable basis for these purposes by the United States of America and the Russian Federation. Joint activities may also be supported, in whole or in part, from funds directly from other sources, including non-government funds and funds from the private sector.
2. In all cases, the activities of, and financial support provided by, the United States of America under this agreement are subject to the availability of appropriated funds. In all cases, the activities of, and financial support provided by, the Russian Federation under this agreement are subject to the availability of appropriated funds.

Article 11

In the event that a Party awards contracts for the acquisition of articles and services, including construction, to implement this agreement, such contracts shall be awarded in accordance with the laws and regulations of that Party.

Article 12

1. Representatives of the US Department of Energy shall have the right upon

reasonable notice to examine and audit the use of any support or assistance provided by the US Government in connection with cooperation under this agreement during the life of this agreement and for three years thereafter. Such examinations may be conducted at sites or locations as agreed to by the Parties' executive agents.

2. The Parties' executive agents shall develop appropriate arrangements for conducting audits and examinations for all work performed within the framework of this agreement.

Article 13

All questions regarding the interpretation or application of this agreement shall be resolved by means consultation between the Parties.

Article 14

1. This agreement shall enter into force on the date of signature, and shall remain in force for five years. The agreement may be extended for successive five-year periods with the written consent of both Parties after joint review before the end of each five-year period. The agreement may be amended by written agreement of the Parties.
2. This agreement may be terminated by either Party by sending written notice through diplomatic channels of its intent to terminate the agreement, in which case the agreement shall terminate six months from the date of the notification.
3. In the event that either Party exercises its right to terminate this agreement, the Parties may agree upon the implementation of settle any outstanding costs by mutual agreement. If this agreement is terminated or expires, the Parties agree that all sensitive information and intellectual property that was made available in the course of the agreement shall continue to be treated in conformance with article 6 of this agreement, unless other arrangements are made by written agreement of the Parties.

Done at Moscow this twenty-fourth day of July, 1998, In duplicate in the English and Russian languages, both texts being equally authentic.

APPENDIX III

For the Government of The United States of America:

For the Government of the Russian Federation:

Annex

To the agreement between the Government of the United States Of America and the Government of the Russian Federation on scientific and technical cooperation in the management of plutonium that has been withdraw from nuclear military programs.

Intellectual Property

Pursuant to Article 6 of this agreement:

The Parties shall ensure adequate and effective protection of intellectual property created or furnished under this agreement and relevant implementing agreements. The Parties agree to notify one another in a timely fashion of any inventions or copyrighted works resulting from scientific and technological work performed under this agreement and to seek protection for such intellectual property in a timely fashion. Rights to such intellectual property shall be allocated as provided in this Annex.

I. Scope

a. This Annex is applicable to all cooperative activities undertaken pursuant to this agreement, except as otherwise specifically agreed by the Parties or their executive agents.

b. For purposed of this agreement, "Intellectual Property" shall have the meaning found in Article 2 of the convention establishing the world intellectual property organization, done at Stockholm, July 14, 1967.

c. This Annex addresses the allocation of rights and interests between the parties. Each Party ensures that the other Party can obtain the rights to intellectual property allocated in accordance with this Annex, by obtaining those rights from its own participants through contracts, license agreements or other legal documents, if necessary; this Annex does not otherwise alter or prejudice the allocation between a Party and its nationals or other legal entities, which shall be determined by that Party's laws and practices.

d. Disputes concerning intellectual property arising under this agreement should be resolved through discussions between the concerned participating institutions, or, if necessary, the Parties or their executive agents. Upon mutual agreement of the Parties, a dispute shall be submitted to an arbitral tribunal for binding arbitration in accordance with the agreement and with the applicable ruled of international law.

e. Termination or expiration of this agreement shall not affect rights or obligations under this Annex.

II Allocation of Rights

a. Each Party shall be entitled to a non-exclusive, irrevocable, royalty-free license in all countries to translate, reproduce, and publicly distribute scientific and technical journal articles, papers, reports, and books directly arising from cooperation under this agreement . All publicly distributed copies of a copyrighted work prepared under this provision shall indicate the names of the authors of the work unless an author explicitly declines to be named.

b. Rights to all forms of intellectual property, other that those rights described in paragraph II. A above, shall be allocated as follows:

(i) Visiting researchers shall receive intellectual property rights under the policies of the host institution. In addition, each visiting researcher named as an inventor or author shall be entitled to awards, policies of the host institution.

(ii) (A) For intellectual property created during joint research, for example, when the Parties, participating institutions, or participating personnel have agreed in advance on the scope of work, each Party shall be entitled to obtain all rights and interests in its own country. Rights and interests in third countries will be determined in implementing agreements. If research is not designated as "Joint Research" in the relevant implementing agreement, rights to intellectual property arising from the research will be allocated in accordance with paragraph II.B. (1) above. In addition, each person named as an inventor or author shall be entitled to receive awards in accordance with the policies of the participating institutions.

(iii) Notwithstanding paragraph II. B. (2) (A) above, if a type of intellectual property is available under the laws of one Party but not the other party, the Party whose laws provide for this type of protection shall be entitled to all rights and interests worldwide. Persons named as inventors or authors of the property shall nonetheless be entitled to awards, bonuses, benefits, or any other rewards in accordance with the policies of the participating institution of the Party obtaining rights.

III Business Confidential Information

In the event that information identified in a timely fashion as business-confidential is furnished or created under this agreement, each Party and its participants shall protect such information in accordance with applicable laws, regulations, and administrative practices. Information may be identified as "Business-Confidential" if a person having the information may derive an economic benefit from it or may obtain a competitive advantage over those who do not have it, the information is not generally known or publicly available from other sources, and the owner has not previously made the information available without imposing in a timely manner an obligation to keep it confidential.

Appendix IV

Agreement between the Government of the United States of America and the Government of the Russian Federation on the Nuclear Cities Initiative

22 September, 1998

The Government of the United States of America and the Government of the Russian Federation, hereafter referred to as the Parties,

Taking into account:

The January 14, 1994, Declartion of the Presidents of the United States of America and the Russian Federation on "Nonproliferation of Weapons of Mass Destruction and the Means of Their Delivery"

The Energy Policy Committee report submitted at the 10th session of the US-Russian Commission on Economic and Technological Cooperation, which was held in March 1998;

The July 24, 1998, Joint Statement on US-Russian Cooperation to Implement the Nuclear Cities Initiative.

Have agreed as follows:

Article 1

The purpose of this Agreement is to create a framework for cooperation in facilitating civilian production that will provide new jobs for workers displaced from enterprises of the nuclear complex in the "nuclear cities" controlled by the Ministry of the Russian Federation for Atomic Energy.

This cooperation shall be in keeping with the Parties' mutual disarmament and non-proliferation efforts.

The Nuclear Cities Initiative complements other bilateral and multilateral agreements to which the United States and the Russian Federation are Parties, and does not supersede them or otherwise affect their terms and conditions.

Article 2

For purposes of this Agreement

1. The term "nuclear cities" shall mean administrative territorial units, as defined under the Law of the Russian Federation on Closed Administrative Territorial Units, that have bodies of local municipal self-government and within which are located nuclear enterprises controlled by the Ministry of the Russian Federation for Atomic Energy, not including the territory of the enterprise itself.
2. Diversification of production shall mean the development, in "nuclear cities," of commercially viable enterprises for civilian production at which displaced employees of the nuclear complex can be employed, with emphasis on former nuclear weapon scientists, engineers, technicians, and other specialists.
3. Civilian production shall mean an enterprise of any form of ownership, with an emphasis on private sector ownership development, that is oriented toward manufacturing or services for civilian use.

Article 3

1. The principal subject areas for the cooperative activities by the Parties may include the following types of activities:
   (a) Sharing experience in diversification of production;
   (b) Facilitating the selection of promising projects for production diversification and creating the conditions that will enable them to be implemented;
   (c) Developing entrepreneurial skills in employees displaced from enterprises of the nuclear complex, training them in how to write a business plan, and facilitating development of such plans;
   (d) Facilitating creation of the conditions necessary for attracting investment in the "nuclear cities" for purposes of implementing the projects within the framework of this Agreement;
   (e) Facilitating the search for investors for production diversification projects, market analysis, and the marketing of products and services produced as a result of the implementation of those projects;

(f) Facilitating access to existing investment mechanisms, including investment funds; and,

(g) Identifying mechanisms for funding of projects under this Agreement.

Article 4

1. The Parties shall designate Executive Agents to carry out the provisions of this Agreement. The Executive Agent for the Russian Federation shall be the Ministry of the Russian Federation for Atomic Energy, and the Executive Agent for the United States of America shall be the US Department of Energy.
2. The Parties shall establish a US-Russian Joint Steering Committee, which shall coordinate work undertaken under this Agreement. Each Party shall designate its own members on the Joint Steering Committee shall be made on the basis of unanimous consent.
3. The tasks of the Joint Steering Committee shall include:
   (a) Development of Joint Action Plans to implement this Agreement;
   (b) Establishment of joint working groups to carry out specific tasks, and coordination of their activities. These groups may be formed based upon specific "nuclear cities" or technical subject depending on the task to be accomplished;
   (c) Coordination and review and the making of recommendations for financing and implementation of projects under this Agreement;
   (d) Resolution of disputes and disagreements that may arise in the course of activities under this Agreement;
   (e) Review of other masters, as the Executive Agents of the Parties may agree in writing, that are within the scope of this Agreement.
4. A detailed plan for implementing specific production diversification project within the framework of the Agreement shall be drawn up in the form of specific implementing arrangements.
5. The Parties' Executive Agents may involve other governmental institutions, auditing, marketing, and law firms, research centers, commercial enterprises, universities, and other organizations of the Parties in joint activities under this Agreement.

Article 5

1. In the implementation of this Agreement, only unclassified information shall be exchanged.
2. In order to prevent access by people and organizations not participating in the implementation of this Agreement to information that is provided by the Parties pursuant to, or is obtained or produced as a result of, implementation of this Agreement and is considered sensitive by the Parties, such information is to be handled as sensitive information. Such information must be clearly designated and marked. The Party transmitting the information will designate information as sensitive in accordance with its laws and regulations. The Party receiving this information shall assign it a designation that provides a degree of protection at least equivalent to that required by the Party that furnished the information.
3. Sensitive information shall be handled in accordance with the laws and regulations of the Party receiving the information, and this information shall not be disclosed or transmitted to a third party not participating in implementation of this Agreement without the written consent of the Party transmitting the information. According to the norms and regulations of the Russian Federation, such information shall be treated as official information with limited distribution and shall be protected appropriately according to the norms and regulations of the United States, such information shall be treated as foreign government information provided in confidence. That information shall be protected appropriately.
4. The Parties shall assure effective protection and allocation of rights to intellectual property transmitted or created under this Agreement, as set forth in this Agreement and in the Annex to this Agreement which forms an integral part of this Agreement.
5. Information transmitted under this Agreement must be used solely in conformance with the provisions of this Agreement.
6. The number of people having access to sensitive information must be limited to the number necessary to implement a specific program under this Agreement and shall be determined by the respective Executive Agent.

Article 6

1. In the event that a Party awards contracts for the acquisition of articles and services, including construction, to implement this Agreement, such contracts shall be awarded in accordance with the laws and regulations of that Party. All activities carried out in the Russian Federation under such contracts shall be performed consistent with Russian Federation law.
2. To the extent necessary for effective implementation of this Agreement, the Executive Agent of the Russian Party shall provide assistance, in accordance with Russian Federation law and the regulatory and legal acts of the federal authorities of the Russian Federation, for timely access for those involved in coordinating and implementing this Agreement to the "nuclear cities" and to sites where activities related to this Agreement are performed.

Article 7

Equipment, supplies, materials, services and activities provided or acquired by the United States of America, its contractors, subcontractors, and their personnel for the implementation of this Agreement are free technical assistance and are thus exempt from customs duties and taxes. The Russian Federation shall take all necessary measures to exempt this equipment shipments, materials, services, and work from all taxes, tariffs, customs duties, and levies of the Russian Federation and its instrumentalities. In carrying out these obligations, the Russian Federation, its ministries, agencies and instrumentalities shall act in accordance with Russian Federation law.

Article 8

1. With the exception of claims against individuals for premeditated damage or injury, the Government of the Russian Federation shall bring no claims or other legal proceedings against the Government of the United States of America and its personnel or its contractors, subcontractors, consultants, suppliers, or subsuppliers or equipment or services at any tier and their personnel, in any court or forum, for any carnage, including indirect, direct, or consequential damage, arising from activities undertaken pursuant to this Agreement, to property owned by the Russian Federation. This

paragraph shall not apply to legal actions brought by the Government of the Russian Federation to enforce the provisions of contracts to which it or a Russian national or other legal entity is a party.

2. With the exception of claims against individuals for premeditated damage or injury, the Government of the Russian Federation shall provide for the adequate defense of , shall indemnify, and shall bring no claims or other legal proceedings against, the Government of the United States of America and its personnel or its contractors, subcontractors, consultants, suppliers, or subsupplers of equipment or services at any tier and their personnel, in connection with third-party claims, in any court or forum, for any injury or damage, including indirect, direct, or consequential injury or damage, arising from activities undertaken pursuant to this Agreement, occurring within or outside the territory of the Russian Federation. Nothing in this paragraph shall be construed as acknowledging the jurisdiction of any court or forum over third-party claims to which this paragraph applies, nor shall it be construed as waiving the sovereign immunity or either Party with respect to third-party claims that may be brought against it.
3. The Parties may, as necessary, conduct consultations regarding claims and legal proceedings concerning this Article.
4. The provisions of this Article shall not prevent the Parties from providing compensation in accordance with their national laws.
5. Nothing in this Article shall be interpreted to prevent legal proceedings or claims against nationals of the Russian Federation or permanent residents of the Russian Federation.

Article 9

1. The joint activities under this Agreement may be supported by funds appropriated for those purposes by the Russian Federation and the United States of America and by materials, equipment, and manpower provided free of charge by them. The joint activities may also be supported partially or wholly directly from other sources, including non-government and private sector funds.
2. In all cases, the activities of, and financial support provided by, the United

States of America under this Agreement are subject to the availability of appropriated funds. In all cases, the activities of, and financial support provided by, the Russian Federation under this Agreement are subject to the availability of appropriated funds.

Article 10

1. Representatives of the United States of America shall have the right, upon giving notice, to perform coordinated inspections of, and to audit, the use of support or assistance provided by the US Government within the framework of cooperation under this Agreement during the life of this Agreement and for three year thereafter. Such inspections may be conducted at sites or locations that are determined by mutual agreement of the Parties' Executive Agents and that are subject to this Agreement.
2. The Parties' Executive Agents shall, within the framework of the Joint Steering Committee, develop appropriate procedures for conducting the inspections of the assistance and support provided within the framework of this Agreement.

Article 11

All questions regarding the interpretation or application of the provision of this Agreement shall be resolved by means of consultation between the Parties.

Article 12

1. This Agreement shall enter into force on the date of signature and shall remain in force for five years. The Agreement may be extended for successive five-year periods with the written consent of both Parties after joint review before the end of each five-year period. The Agreement may be amended by written agreement of the Parties.
2. This Agreement may be terminated by either Party by sending written notice through diplomatic channels of its intent to terminate the Agreement, in which case the Agreement shall terminate six months from the date of the notification.
3. If the Agreement is terminated by either Party, the Parties may agree upon

the full implementation of existing contracts and projects and will settle any outstanding costs by mutual agreement. If this Agreement is terminated or expires, the Parties agree that all sensitive information and intellectual property obtained or created in the course of implementation of the Agreement shall continue to be treated in conformance with Article 5 of this Agreement, unless other arrangements are made by written agreement of the Parties.

Done at Vienna this 22nd day of September, 1998 in two copies each, in the English and in Russian languages, each text being equally authentic.

For the Government of the United States:
For the Government of the Russian Federation:

Appendix V

The Weapons Of Mass Destruction And Their Delivery Systems (Prohibition Of Unlawful Activities) Act, 2005

No. 21 of 2005

[6th June, 2005]

An Act to prohibit unlawful activities, in relation to weapons of mass destruction and their delivery systems and for matters connected therewith or incidental thereto.

WHEREAS India is determined to safeguard its national security as a Nuclear Weapon State;

AND WHEREAS India is committed not to transfer nuclear weapons or other nuclear explosive devices, or to transfer control over such weapons or explosive devices, and not in any way to assist, encourage, or induce any other country to manufacture nuclear weapons or other nuclear explosive devices;

AND WHEREAS India is committed to prevent a non-State actor and a terrorist from acquiring weapons of mass destruction and their delivery systems;

AND WHEREAS India is committed to the objective of global nuclear disarmament;

AND WHEREAS India is committed to its obligations as a State Party to the Convention on the Prohibition of the Development, Production, Stockpiling and Use of Chemical Weapons and on their Destruction and the Convention on the Prohibition of the Development, Production and Stockpiling of Bacteriological (Biological) and Toxic Weapons and on their Destruction;

AND WHEREAS India is exercising controls over the export of chemicals, organisms, materials, equipment and technologies in relation to weapons of mass destruction and their delivery systems under other relevant Acts;

AND WHEREAS it is considered necessary to provide for integrated legal measures to exercise controls over the export of materials, equipment and technologies and to prohibit unlawful activities in relation to weapons of mass destruction and their means of delivery.

BE it enacted by Parliament in the Fifty-sixth Year of the Republic of India as follows:-

1. **Short title and commencement.**- (1) This Act may be called the Weapons of Mass Destruction and their Delivery Systems (Prohibition of Unlawful Activities) Act, 2005.

   (2) It shall come into force on such date as the Central Government may, by notification in the Official Gazette, appoint.

2. **Act in addition to other laws.**-Save as otherwise expressly provided in this Act, the provisions of this Act shall be in addition to any other relevant Act for the time being in force in relation to any matter covered under this Act.

3. **Extent and application.** - (1) It extends to the whole of India including its Exclusive Economic Zone.

   (2) Every person shall be liable to punishment under this Act for every act or omission contrary to the provisions thereof, of which he is held guilty in India.

   (3) Any person who commits an offence beyond India, which is punishable under this Act, shall be dealt with according to the provisions of this Act in the same manner as if such act had been committed in India.

   (4) The provisions of this Act shall also apply to -

   (a) citizens of India outside India;

   (b) companies or bodies corporate, registered or incorporated in India or having their associates, branches or subsidiaries, outside India;

   (c) any ship, aircraft or other means of transport registered in India or outside India, wherever it may be;

   (d) foreigners while in India;

   (e) persons in the service of the Government of India, within and beyond India.

   (5) Notwithstanding the applicability of the provisions of any other Central Act relating to any activity provided herein, the provisions of this Act shall apply to export, transfer, re-transfer, transit and trans-shipment of material, equipment or technology of any description as are identified, designated, categorised or considered necessary by the Central Government, as pertinent or relevant to India as a Nuclear Weapon State, or to the national

security of India, or to the furtherance of its foreign policy or its international obligations under any bilateral, multilateral or international treaty, Covenant, Convention or arrangement relating to weapons of mass destruction or their means of delivery, to which India is a Party.

4. **Definitions.** - In this Act, unless the context otherwise requires,-

(a) "biological weapons" are-

(i) microbial or other biological agents, or toxins whatever their origin or method of production, of types and in quantities that have no justification for prophylactic, protective or other peaceful purposes; and

(ii) weapons, equipment or delivery systems specially designed to use such agents or toxins for hostile purposes or in armed conflict;

(b) "brought in transit" means to bring goods from any country into India by land, air, or amphibious means of transportation, where the goods are to be taken out from India on the same conveyance on which they are brought into India without any landing in India, but does not include a conveyance in innocent passage through Indian territory, Indian territorial waters or Indian airspace of a foreign conveyance carrying goods.

Explanation I.-A conveyance is a foreign conveyance if it is not registered in India.

Explanation II.-A conveyance is in "innocent passage" if it is not engaged in relevant activity and passes through or above Indian territorial waters or airspace without stopping or anchoring in India;

(c) "chemical weapons" means,-

(i) the toxic chemicals and their precursors, except where intended for-

(a) industrial, agricultural, research, medical, pharmaceutical or other peaceful purposes;

(b) protective purposes, namely those purposes directly related to protection against toxic chemicals and to protection against chemical weapons;

(c) military purposes not connected with the use of chemical weapons and not dependent on the use of the toxic properties of chemicals as a method of warfare; or

(d) law enforcement including domestic riot control purposes; as long as the types and quantities are consistent with such purposes;

(ii) the munitions and devices, specifically designed to cause death or other harm through the toxic properties of those toxic chemicals specified in sub-clause (i), which would be released as a result of the employment of such munitions and devices; and

(iii) any equipment specifically designed for use directly in connection with the employment of munitions and devices specified in sub-clause (ii),

together or separately;

(d) "export" shall have the meaning assigned to this expression in the Foreign Trade (Development and Regulation) Act, 1992 (22 of 1992);

(e) "fissile material" and "radioactive material" shall have the meanings assigned to these expressions in the Atomic Energy Act, 1962 (33 of 1962);

(f) "item" means materials, equipment, and technology, of any description, notified under this Act or any other Act related to relevant activity;

(g) "non-State actor" is a person or entity not acting under the lawful authority of any country;

(h) "nuclear weapon or other nuclear explosive device" means any nuclear weapon or other nuclear explosive device as may be determined by the Central Government, whose determination in the matter shall be final;

(i) "public domain" means domain that has no restrictions upon dissemination of information within or from it; the existence of any legal rights to intellectual property in that information does not remove such information from being in public domain;

(j) "relevant activity" means,-

(i) the development, production, handling, operation, maintenance, storage or dissemination of a nuclear, chemical or biological weapon; or

(ii) the development, production, maintenance, storage or dissemina-tion of missiles specially designed for delivering any such weapon;

(k) "re-transfer" means transfer of any item notified under this Act from any country or entity to which it has been exported from India, to yet another country or entity;

(l) "technology" means any information (including information embodied in software) other than information in the public domain, that is capable of being used in-

(i) the development, production or use of any goods or software;

(ii) the development of, or the carrying out of, an industrial or commercial activity or the provision of a service of any kind.

Explanation.-When technology is described wholly or partly by reference to the uses to which it (or the goods to which it relates) may be put, it shall include services which are provided or used, or which are capable of being used, in the development, production or use of such technology or goods;

(m) "terrorist" shall have the meaning assigned to this expression in the Unlawful Activities (Prevention) Act, 1967 (37 of 1967);

(n) "trans-shipment" means to remove goods from the conveyance on which they were brought into India and to place the goods on the same or another conveyance for the purpose of taking them out of India, where these acts are carried out on a "through bill of lading", "through airway bill" or "through manifest".

Explanation.- "through bill of lading", "through airway bill" and "through manifest" means respectively a bill of lading, airway bill and manifest, for the consignment of goods from a place outside India to a destination which is also outside India without a consignee in India;

(o) "unlawful" means without the authority of the Central Government and the expression "unlawfully" shall be construed accordingly;

(p) "weapons of mass destruction" means any biological, chemical or nuclear weapons.

5. **Power to identify, designate, categorise or regulate certain activities.-**
   (1) The Central Government may identify, designate, categorise or regulate, the export, transfer, re-transfer, trans-shipment, or transit of any item related to relevant activity in such manner as may be prescribed.
   (2) The Central Government may, by order published in the Official Gazette, designate or notify any item related to relevant activity for the purposes of this Act.
6. **Power to appoint Advisory Committees.-** For the purposes of this Act, the Central Government may appoint such Advisory Committees as it deems fit, and may appoint to them persons to exercise such powers and perform such duties as the Central Government may, by rules, prescribe.
7. **Delegation of powers.-** (1) Subject to the provisions of this Act and any other law for the time being in force, related to relevant activity, the Central Government shall have the power to direct or assign to any authority, in such manner as it may deem appropriate, such powers as may be necessary to implement the provisions of this Act.
   (2) The Central Government may appoint a Licensing Authority and an Appellate Authority and make provisions relating to such authority and for licensing in such manner and in such form, as the Central Government may, by rules, prescribe.
   (3) Without prejudice to the generality of the provisions contained in this Act, the authorities and mechanisms provided under other relevant Acts shall continue to deal with matters covered under those Acts:
   Provided that in case of any doubt as to whether a matter falls within the scope of such relevant Acts or under this Act, the decision of the Central Government thereon shall be final.
8. **Prohibition relating to weapons of mass destruction.-** (1) No person shall unlawfully manufacture, acquire, possess, develop or transport a nuclear weapon or other nuclear explosive device and their means of delivery.
   (2) No person shall unlawfully transfer, directly or indirectly, to any one a nuclear weapon or other nuclear explosive device, or transfer control over such a weapon, knowing it to be a nuclear weapon or other nuclear explosive device.

(3) No person shall unlawfully manufacture, acquire, possess, develop or transport a biological or chemical weapon or their means of delivery.

(4) No person shall unlawfully transfer, directly or indirectly, to any one biological or chemical weapons.

(5) No person shall unlawfully transfer, directly or indirectly, to any one missiles specially designed for the delivery of weapons of mass destruction.

9. **Prohibition relating to non-State actor or terrorist.**- No person shall, directly or indirectly, transfer to a non-State actor or terrorist, any material, equipment and technology notified under this Act or any other Act related to relevant activity:

Provided that such transfer made to a non-State actor shall not include a transfer made as such to any person acting under lawful authority in India.

10. **Prohibition as regards intimidating acts.**- No person shall transfer, acquire, possess, or transport fissile or radioactive material, which is intended to be used to cause, or in a threat to cause, death or serious injury or damage to property for the purpose of intimidating people or a section of the people in India or in any foreign country, or compelling the Government of India or the Government of a foreign country or an international organisation or any other person to do so or abstain from doing any act.

11. **Prohibition on export.**- No person shall export any material, equipment or technology knowing that such material, equipment or technology is intended to be used in the design or manufacture of a biological weapon, chemical weapon, nuclear weapon or other nuclear explosive device, or in their missile delivery systems.

12. **Prohibition on brokering.**- No person who is a resident in India shall, for a consideration under the terms of an actual or implied contract, knowingly facilitate the execution of any transaction which is prohibited or regulated under this Act:

Provided that a mere carriage, without knowledge, of persons, goods or technology, or provision of services, including by a public or private carrier of goods, courier, tele-communication, postal service provider or financial service provider, shall not be an offence for the purposes of this section.

13. **Regulation of export, transfer, retransfer, transit and transshipment.**- (1) No item notified under this Act shall be exported, transferred, re-transferred, brought in transit or transhipped except in accordance with the provisions of this Act or any other relevant Act.

(2) Any transfer of technology of an item whose export is prohibited under this Act or any other relevant Act relating to relevant activity shall be prohibited.

(3) When any technology is notified under this Act or any other relevant Act, as being subject to transfer controls, the transfer of such technology shall be restricted to the extent notified thereunder.

Explanation.- The transfer of technology may take place through either or both of the following modes of transfer, namely:-

(a) by a person or from a place within India to a person or place outside India;

(b) by a person or from a place outside India to a person, or a place, which is also outside India (but only where the transfer is by, or within the control of, person, who is a citizen of India, or any person who is a resident in India).

(4) The Central Government may notify any item as being subject to the provisions of this Act, whether or not it is covered under any other relevant Act; and when such item is exhibited, sold, supplied or transferred to any foreign entity or a foreigner who is resident, operating, visiting, studying, or conducting research or business within the territorial limits of India, or in its airspace or Exclusive Economic Zone, it shall constitute an offence.

14. **Offences and penalties.**- Any person who contravenes, or attempts to contravene or abets, the provisions of section 8 or section 10 of this Act, shall be punishable with imprisonment for a term which shall not be less than five years but which may extend to imprisonment for life, and shall also be liable to fine.

15. **Punishment for aiding non-State actor or terrorist.**- (1) Any person who, with intent to aid any non-State actor or terrorist, contravenes the provisions of section 9 of this Act, shall be punishable with imprisonment for a term which shall not be less than five years but which may extend to

imprisonment for life, and shall also be liable to fine.

(2) Any person who, with intent to aid any non-State actor or terrorist, attempts to contravene or abets, or does any act preparatory to contravention of sub-section (1), shall be deemed to have contravened that provision and the provision of sub-section (1) shall apply subject to the modification that the reference to "imprisonment for life" therein shall be construed as a reference to "imprisonment for ten years".

(3) While determining the punishment under this section, the court shall take into consideration whether the accused had the knowledge about the transferee being a non-State actor or not.

16. **Punishment for unauthorized export.**- (1) Any person who knowingly contravenes, abets or attempts to contravene, the provisions of sub-section (4) of section 13 of this Act, shall be punishable with fine which shall not be less than three lakh rupees and which may extend to twenty lakh rupees.

(2) If any person is again convicted of the same offence under sub-section (1), then he shall be punishable for the second and every subsequent offence with imprisonment for a term which shall not be less than six months but which may extend to five years and shall also be liable to fine.

17. **Punishment for violation of other provisions of the Act.**- (1) Where any person contravenes, or abets or attempts to contravene, any provision of this Act other than the provisions under sections 8, 9, 10 and sub-section (4) of section 13 of this Act, he shall be punishable with imprisonment for a term which shall not be less than six months but which may extend to five years and shall also be liable to fine.

(2) If any person is again convicted of the same offence under sub-section (1), then he shall be punishable for the second and every subsequent offence with imprisonment for a term which shall not be less than one year but which may extend to seven years and shall also be liable to fine.

18. **Penalty for using false or making forged documents, etc.**- Where any person signs or uses, or causes to be signed or used, any declaration, statement or document submitted to the competent authority knowing or having reason to believe that such declaration, statement or document is forged or tampered with or is false in any material particular, and relates to

items notified under this Act or any other relevant Act, including those related to relevant activity, he shall be punishable with fine which shall not be less than five lakh rupees or five times the value of the materials, equipment, technology or services, whichever is more.

19. **Punishment for offences with respect to which no provision has been made.**- Whoever contravenes any other provision of this Act or any rule or order made thereunder for which no specific punishment is provided, shall be punishable with imprisonment for a term which may extend to one year, or with fine, or with both.

20. **Offences by companies.**- (1) Where an offence under this Act has been committed by a company, every person who at the time the offence was committed was in charge of, and was responsible to, the company for the conduct of the business of the company as well as the company, shall be deemed to be guilty of the offence and shall be liable to be proceeded against and punished accordingly:

Provided that nothing contained in this sub-section shall render any such person liable to any punishment, if he proves that the offence was committed without his knowledge or that he had exercised all due diligence to prevent the commission of such offence.

(2) Notwithstanding anything contained in sub-section (1), where any offence under this Act has been committed by a company and it is proved that the offence has been committed with the consent or connivance of, or is attributable to, any neglect on the part of, any director, manager, secretary or other officer of the company, such director, manager, secretary or other officer shall be deemed to be guilty of that offence and shall be liable to be proceeded against and punished accordingly.

Explanation.-For the purposes of this section-

(a) "company" means any corporate body and includes a firm and other association of individuals; and

(b) "director", in relation to a firm, means a partner in the firm.

21. **Cognizance of offences.**- No Court shall take cognizance of any offence under this Act without the previous sanction of the Central Government or any officer authorised by the Central Government in this behalf.

APPENDIX V

22. **Bar of jurisdiction of civil courts.**- No action or proceedings taken under section 5 and sub-sections (1) and (2) of section 7 of this Act by the Central Government or any officer authorised by it in this behalf shall be called in question in any civil court in any suit or application or by way of appeal or revision, and no injunction shall be granted by any civil court or other authority in respect of any action taken or to be taken in pursuance of any power conferred under those provisions.

23. **Effect of other laws.**- (1) The provisions of this Act shall have effect notwithstanding anything inconsistent therewith contained in any enactment other than this Act or any other instrument having effect by virtue of any enactment other than this Act.

    (2) Where any act or omission constitutes an offence punishable under this Act and also under any other relevant Act, then the offender found guilty of such offence shall be liable to be punished under that Act which imposes a greater punishment.

24. **Protection of action taken in good faith.**- No suit, prosecution or other legal proceeding shall lie against the Central Government or any officer or authority of the Central Government or any other authority on whom powers have been conferred pursuant to this Act, for anything which is in good faith done or purported to be done in pursuance of this Act or any rule or order made thereunder.

25. **Special provisions as to Central Government.**- Nothing in this Act shall affect the activities of the Central Government in the discharge of its functions relating to the security or the defence of India.

26. **Power to make rules.**- (1) The Central Government may, by notification, make rules to carry out the provisions of this Act.

    (2) In particular and without prejudice to the generality of the foregoing power, such rules may provide for all or any of the following matters, namely:-

    (a) manner of regulating any item related to relevant activity under sub-section (1) of section 5;

    (b) appointment of Advisory Committees, their powers and duties under section 6;

(c) appointment of Licensing and Appellate Authority and the manner of licensing under sub-section (2) of section 7; and

(d) any other matter which has to be, or may be, prescribed.

(3) Every rule made under this Act shall be laid, as soon as may be after it is made, before each House of Parliament, while it is in session for a total period of thirty days which may be comprised in one session or in two or more successive sessions, and if, before the expiry of the session immediately following the session or the successive sessions aforesaid, both Houses agree in making any modification in the rule or both Houses agree that the rule should not be made, the rule shall thereafter have effect only in such modified form or be of no effect, as the case may be; so, however, that any such modification or annulment shall be without prejudice to the validity of anything previously done under that rule.

27. **Power to remove difficulties.**- (1) If any difficulty arises in giving effect to the provisions of this Act, the Central Government may, by order published in the Official Gazette, make such provisions, not inconsistent with the provisions of this Act, as may appear to be necessary for removing the difficulty:

Provided that no order shall be made under this section after the expiry of the period of two years from the date of commencement of this Act.

(2) Every order made under this section shall be laid, as soon as may be after it is made, before each House of Parliament.

T.K. VISWANATHAN,
Secy. to the Govt. of India

Appendix VI

Fig. 1

DAE - Emergency Response Centres

1) Mumbai -BARC (Nodal ERC)
2) Tarapur
3) Kakrapar
4) Kota
5) Jaipur
6) Narora
7) Shillong
8) Jaduguda
9) Kolkata
10) Nagpur
11) Hyderabad
12) Kaiga
13) Bangalore
14) Kalpakkam
15) Alwaye
16) New Delhi
17) Kudamkulam
18) Indore

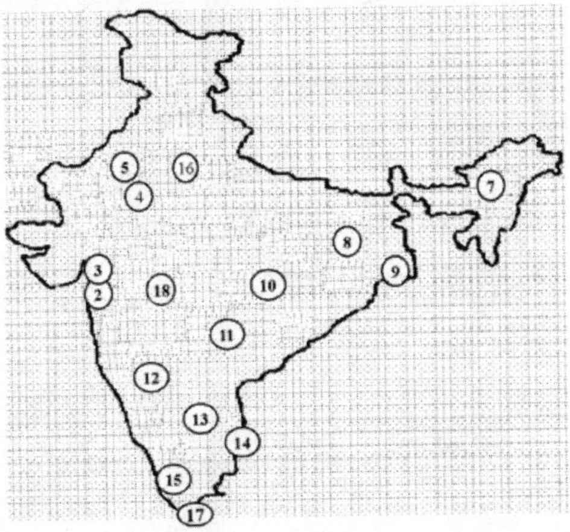

Fig. 2

Aerial Gamma Spectrometry System (AGSS) developed in BARC has demonstrated its capability for online assessment of radiological impact during many aerial survey exercises with Mi17 helicopters over 'simulated contamination.'

Fig. 3

Online display during an aerial survey exercise conducted by BARC over 'simulated radioactive contamination' by installing the AGSS in a Mi17 helicopter.

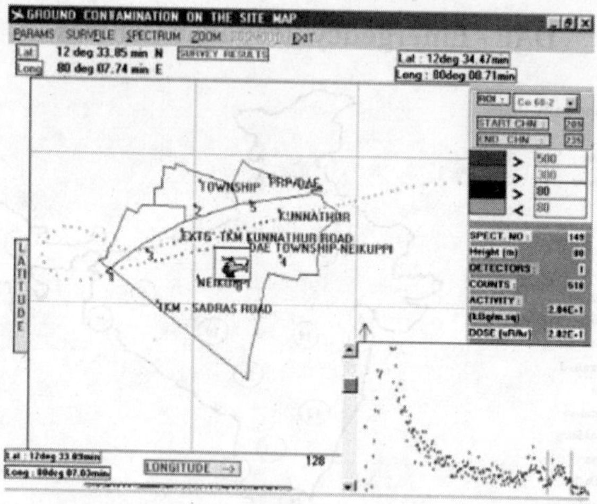

Fig. 4

Compact Aerial Radiation Monitoring System (CARMS): System developed in BARC for remote aerial radiation monitoring.

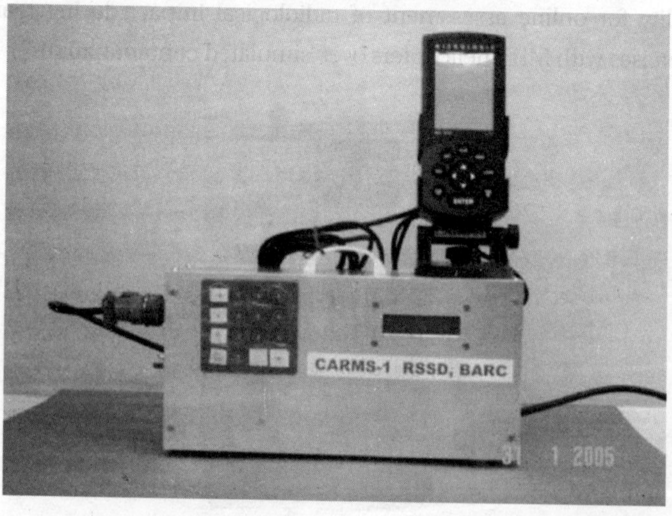

APPENDIX VI

Fig. 5

Solar-backed-GSM based environmental radiation monitor under the Indian Environmental Radiation Monitoring Network (IERMON).

Fig. 6

Display on a satellite imagery- mapping of a 'contaminated area' which can be based on an aerial survey using AGSS or the isodose curves predicted by dispersion models.